between

a girl's guide to life

between

a girl's guide to life

by vicki courtney

between:
a girl's guide to life

Copyright © 2006 by Vicki Courtney
All rights reserved.
Printed in the United States of America
Published by B&H Publishing Group
Nashville, Tennessee

Ten-digit ISBN: 0-8054-4193-X
Thirteen-digit ISBN: 978-0-8054-4193-2

Dewey Decimal Classification: 170

Subject Heading: VIRTUE \ TEENAGERS \ GIRLS

Unless otherwise noted, all Scripture is taken from the Holman Christian Standard Bible®
Copyright © 1999, 2000, 2002, 2003 by Holman Bible Publishers. Used by permission. Other
versions include: NIV, New International Version, copyright © 1973, 1978, 1984 by International
Bible Society; NASB, New American Standard Bible, © Lockman Foundation, 1960, 1962, 1968,
1971, 1972, 1973, 1975, 1977, 1995, used by permission, NLT, New Living Translation, copyright © 1996, used by permission of Tyndale House Publishers, Inc., Wheaton, IL 60189 USA. All
rights reserved. *The Message*, the New Testament in Contemporary English, © 1993, by Eugene
H. Peterson, published by NavPress, Colorado Springs, CO; and CEV, the Contemporary English
Version, © American Bible Society 1991, 1992; used by permission.

1 2 3 4 5 6 7 8 9 10   10 09 08 07 06

CHECK THIS OUT:

author web sites:

Virtuousreality.com: features online magazines for preteens, teens, and mothers.

Virtuousreality.com/events: provides a schedule of upcoming Yada Yada and Yada Yada Junior events for girls ages third through twelfth grades and mothers; also information about how you can bring an event to your area.

Vickicourtney.com: to view Vicki Courtney's current speaking schedule or to find information about inviting her to speak.

Virtuealert.com: educates parents, youth workers and pastors about the latest trends in teen culture and equips them with the knowledge to protect teens from potential dangers.

other books by vicki courtney from B&H:

Your Girl: Raising a Godly Daughter in an Ungodly World

Yada Yada: A Devotional Journal for Moms

More Than Just Talk: A Journal for Girls

The Virtuous Woman: Shattering the Superwoman Myth

TeenVirtue: Real Issues, Real Life . . . A Teen Girl's Survival Guide

TeenVirtue 2: A Teen Girl's Guide to Relationships

Your Boy: Raising a Godly Son in an Ungodly World

TABLE OF CONTENTS

CHAPTER 2: OTHERS

CHAPTER 3: GOD

ABOUT THE AUTHORS

VICKI COURTNEY is the founder of Virtuous Reality Ministries, which reaches more than 150,000 girls and moms a year through events, an online magazine for teen girls (virtuousreality.com), and other resources. She is a national speaker and the best-selling author of *TeenVirtue: Real Issues, Real Life . . . A Teen Girl's Survival Guide.* She lives in Austin, Texas, with her husband, Keith, and three children, Ryan, Paige, and Hayden. To find out more, visit her website at VickiCourtney.com.

SUSIE DAVIS communicates with girls and women of all ages, including Virtuous Reality sponsored Yada Yada events for teen girls and their mothers. In addition, she is the author of *The Time of Your Life: Finding God's Rest in Your Busy Schedule.* She lives in Austin, Texas, with her husband, Will, and three children, Will III, Emily, and Sara. To find out more, visit her website at SusieDavisMinistries.com.

WHITNEY PROSPERI has a heart for girls and girls' ministry. She is the author of *Life Style: Real Perspectives from Radical Women in the Bible*, a twelve-week Bible study for middle and high school girls, as well as *Girls Ministry 101*, published by Youth Specialties. She lives in Tyler, Texas, with her husband, Randy, and daughters Annabelle and Libby.

WHEN I WAS A LITTLE GIRL (much younger than you), I thought that God lived in the moon. My mom told me that he lived in heaven and when I asked where heaven was, she would just point up to the sky. I guess since the moon was the highest object I could see in the sky, I decided that's where God lives. When the moon was full, I was pretty sure I could see him curled up in the bottom left part of it, resting after a busy day of watching over the whole world. Then one day I went to school and learned that the shadowy part of the moon that I had thought was God was really caused by hot lava that had poured out long ago on the moon's surface. That part of the moon looks darker than the rest of the moon because it doesn't reflect the sunlight anymore. So, if that wasn't God, where was he? It was then that I began to wonder if there really was a God. I wanted to be able to see him and know he was there. Most of all, I wanted to believe that he was watching over me—if not from the moon, somewhere else.

Well, the good news is, there is a God and he's watching over you this very minute! Even though you can't see him, he's only a prayer away. In fact, get this: he never sleeps! You can call on him any minute of the day and he will hear you. He cares about your problems . . . like pesky little brothers, best friends who get new best friends, girls who whisper behind your back, bodies that grow too fast (or too slow!), and even that boy in your class who can be confusing, and annoying, but at the same time, kind of cute. Yes, God cares.

Sometimes growing up can be tough, but God never meant for you to feel alone in the journey. *Between* is a survival guide to help you in your growing up journey. It talks about many of the issues girls your age will face in the years leading up to being a teenager. Best of all, it lets you know what God thinks about it all. I've even included fun "Just Between Us" questions for you to answer on your own or with a small group of girls. In fact, I wish *Between* had been around when I was your age. After my "God lives in the moon" story, you can see why I could have used a little help. Next time you see a full moon, think of me, laugh your head off, and then thank God for watching over you every minute of every day. ☺

—VICKI COURTNEY

INTRODUCTION

CHAPTER 1:
YOU

Little Miss Popular

by Vicki Courtney

I will never, ever forget the day I was voted the most popular girl in the sixth grade. I couldn't believe it. There were several other girls I thought for sure would be picked, but my classmates chose me! When I found out the results, my heart felt like it was going to jump right out of my body and do a little dance right there in the middle of class. I know that's kinda funny to imagine, but being voted most popular made my heart feel good. Now I'm not talking about plain ole good. I'm talking about no school- stay up late-watch your favorite movie- eat your favorite ice cream kind of good.

Because I was voted most popular, I got tons of calls to spend the night and invitations to birthday parties. I even got asked out by the most popular boy in class! Maybe that is when I became addicted to being popular. "Addicted" is a way of saying you are hooked on something—like you can't live without it. You might be addicted to chocolate or old *Full House* reruns. Some moms and girls are addicted to shopping. You get the picture. Well, when I was your age, I was hooked on being popular. I remember at the end of the year when we would get our yearbooks and have a yearbook sign- ing party. I couldn't wait to go home and read all the things my friends would write in my yearbook. Every time one of my class- mates used words like *pretty* or *popular* to describe me, my heart would beat fast. When they said how good I was at track and gymnastics, it beat even faster. My

> ## When I was your age, I was hooked on being popular. I realized how great it felt to have people like me.

Pretty and *Talented*

heart did that same dance all over again! I realized how great it felt to have people like me.

This addiction to being popular went on for years and years, and my life became all about keeping the title of "Most Popular." I kept thinking to myself, *What if they stop liking me? What if the phone stops ringing? What if the boys stop liking me and don't ask me out?" "What if I'm not popular next year, or the next, or the next?* And then my worst fear happened. Years later I was "Sort of Popular" but not "Most Popular." "Most Popular" only lasted for a short time, and there were other girls who stepped in and took my place. Since I was kind of addicted to popularity and only felt good about myself when I had it, I didn't feel very good about myself when I lost it..

You may not look like a supermodel, but in God's eyes you are "remarkably and wonderfully made" (Psalm 139:14). You are his creation, and you are beautiful.

Why do you think popularity is important to most girls? Having been one of those girls who cared (too much) about being popular, I think I know why.

You know how in math class you learned to do equations like this: 1 + 2 + 3 = 6? In that equation, to get the answer 6, you had to add 1 and 2 and 3 together. Sometimes we can think of our worth, or what we feel about ourselves, like a math equation. We feel like we have to add together a bunch of things to feel good about ourselves. Let me show you what I mean:

Being pretty + Being popular + Being talented = Feeling good about myself

Remember how my heart beat faster and faster when I knew people thought I was pretty, or good at track, or popular? Remember how I felt sad when those things went away? Well, that's the problem with this math equation. If you take one or more of those things away (being pretty, being popular, being talented), it doesn't add up anymore, and you don't feel good about yourself. In fact, here is what my math equation looked like in ninth grade:

I have a big nose + I didn't get invited to Missy's party + I didn't make cheerleader = Feeling crummy about myself

Now that I'm older, I realize that my math equation was all wrong. I shouldn't have based my worth (how I felt about myself) on being pretty, popular, or talented. Sure,

everyone wants to look good, be talented, and be liked by others, but it becomes a problem when those things become so important that we can't feel good about ourselves without them. You see, none of those things stay the same forever and ever. But you know

Worth = what God thinks of me

I'm Worthy

really worthy

what does? How God thinks of us. That is something that will never change!

You may not look like a supermodel, but in God's eyes you are "remarkably and wonderfully made" (Psalm 139:14). You are his creation, and you are beautiful. The next time you look in the mirror and begin to think differently, smile and walk away. Or, if you feel funny about your body as it changes, remember that God made you perfect just the way you are! God doesn't make mistakes.

If you care a lot about what others think, remind yourself of how God thinks of you. It's really all that matters. There is nothing you can do to make God stop loving you. Even at times when you have done something wrong, God still loves you. If that truth doesn't make your heart beat faster, then I don't know what will!

I want you to notice in God's equation, nothing is said about being talented or "doing" anything. That's because it is impossible for God to love us more than he already does—even if we do a zillion good deeds.

It's time to think about yourself in a whole new way. You are priceless to God. You know how moms will sometimes carry around pictures of their kids? I've heard it said that God loves us so much that if he had a wallet, our pictures would be in it. Pretty amazing! If you ask me, it's a lot better than being voted the most popular girl in the sixth grade. The truth is, you ARE popular—with the God of the universe! ✳

JUST BETWEEN US

1. Have you believed the equation below?
Being pretty + Being popular + Being talented = Feeling good about myself

2. If so, which one means the most to you? Being pretty, popular, or talented? Why?

3. Why is it wrong to believe in this equation?

4. How does it make you feel to know how God feels about you?

5. Why does God's equation last longer over time?

6. What are some things you can do when you are not feeling good about yourself? (Example: Memorize Psalm 139:14 and imagine your picture in God's wallet.)

thanking God for your bod

by Vicki Courtney

Have you ever stood in front of your mirror and huffed under your breath, "I don't like my body?" Have you ever wished you had longer legs, straighter hair, or stronger muscles for sports? Or maybe you've wished you didn't have freckles, fair skin, or that weird birthmark. Do you dream of being heavier, thinner, taller, or shorter? If you have answered yes to any of these, you are not alone. We can all fall into the "I wish" trap. You know what I'm talking about. "I wish I was as skinny as so and so." "I wish I was as pretty as she is." "I wish my nose wasn't so big." "I wish my ears didn't stick out so much." I wish, I wish, I wish. You get the picture.

What causes the "I wish" trap? Sometimes we compare ourselves to other people. The crazy thing is that those "other people" are probably also comparing themselves to other people! Or maybe you compare yourself to girls you see on television or in magazines who look perfect. You know the ones I'm talking about. They have perfect hair that is never messed up. They have perfect skin and perfect legs and perfect everything. Well, let me tell you a little secret about that. They are really not as perfect as they look. For one thing, they are wearing a lot of makeup, and they had it put on by a professional makeup artist who knows how to make it look perfect. Most of the models in the magazines have had their pictures "touched up." What that means is that you can make someone in a picture

Have you ever stood in front of your mirror and huffed under your breath, "I don't like my body"?

look perfect. You can take away freckles or make a model's legs look skinnier. You can even change a model's hair color or the color of the shirt she is wearing in the picture. If you wanted to, you could add silly Mickey Mouse ears on her head and give her a mustache. In real life, she really looks more like you and me.

BEFORE AFTER

An example of a "touched-up" photo. The girl's acne has been removed, her hair looks combed, her shirt color has been changed, and now her eyes are even blue! You might think that she's perfect, but she's not!

The true test is to be able to look at yourself in the mirror and confidently say, "I praise you because I am fearfully and wonderfully made; your works are wonderful, I know that full well." (Psalm 139:14)

I wish I had known that when I was your age. I always compared myself to other people, and I had a hard time accepting the body God gave me. I fell into the "I wish trap." I wanted to look in the mirror and like what I saw, but I couldn't because I was always wishing for something else. Today, many years later, I like my reflection in the mirror. So, what's my secret, you ask? I realized that God doesn't make junk and that every time I wished for this or that, I was basically telling God that I wasn't happy with the body he gave me.

Of course I'm not saying it's OK to eat five bags of Oreos and become a lazy couch potato. I'm talking about accepting your body shape for what it is: short, tall, big-boned, or petite. Even if you are currently overweight or underweight, you can still have a goal to reach a healthy weight range and at the same time accept the body type God gave you.

The true test is to be able to look at yourself in the mirror and confidently say, "I praise you because I am fearfully and wonderfully made; your works are wonderful, I know that full well" (Psalm 139:14 NIV). If you can't say it and mean it, consider putting the verse on your mirror as a reminder and say it every day. Pray and ask God to help you believe it. God knew exactly what he was doing when he created you. ✳

1. Who are some people you sometimes compare yourself to? What would be on your "I wish" list when it comes to your body?

2. Do you think God made any mistakes when he made your body? Why or why not?

3. Take some paper and make a list of things you like about your body.

4. Now take the list of things you like about your body, pray and ask God to help you add to it until you can list everything about your body! You will begin to see your body as God does—perfect!

God doesn't make junk!

"Pwiddy Gulls"

by Vicki Courtney

My daughter was one of those beautiful babies who got lots and lots of attention wherever she went. She was teeny-tiny for her age and had beautiful fair skin, blonde curly hair, blue eyes, and a sparkling personality. When she started walking, people often commented that she looked like a walking baby doll. Everywhere we went, she attracted oohs and aahs. In the beginning, I loved the attention she got and would just smile proudly when people commented on how adorably cute she was.

When God looks at her, he doesn't look at her outer appearance— he looks at her heart. ♥

Of course, she was just a baby and didn't realize why she was getting the attention—until one day when she was about three years old. I remember we were walking along a sidewalk and she caught a glimpse of her reflection in a shop window and said, "Oooh, pwiddy gull." At the time, I thought it was perfectly adorable and thought to myself, *Wow, this kid is going to grow up and feel really good about herself!*

About a year later, however, I realized we had a problem. She was four years old and in preschool. It was picture day at her school, and we put on her prettiest dress with the matching hair ribbon.

When I dropped her off at the door that morning, her teacher said, "Paige, you are such a pretty girl." And instead of saying thank you, my child brushed by her teacher with a sideways glance and said, "I know. Everyone tells me that." I was so embarrassed! After that, I quit making comments about her outer beauty and tried to compliment her more on her inner beauty. I would say things like, "Paige, you are so giving to let your friend have the cupcake with the most icing," or, "Paige, you are sweet to read your little brother a book." I didn't want her to grow up thinking that she was only special if she was a "pwiddy gull." Besides, everyone knows that "pwiddy gulls" don't always grow up to be "pwiddy BIG girls," right?

The Bible says that **"beauty does not last" (Proverbs 31:30 NLT).** I'm sure you've noticed by now that as people get older, their bodies start to look older. That's why I feel sorry for really pretty people who only feel good about themselves because they are pretty. Someday they will look in the mirror and see wrinkles on their forehead and around their eyes, and they will notice that their hair is getting gray. If they haven't learned that beauty really comes from the inside, they will look in the mirror and not like the person staring back at them.

Today my daughter is in high school, and she is still a very "pwiddy gull." Most importantly, she is "pwiddy" on the inside. My daughter knows that when God looks at her, he doesn't look at her outer appearance—he looks at her heart. She knows that the best beauty secret is to see herself through God's eyes. Remember the Bible verse that talked about beauty not lasting? Well the last part of that verse has the best beauty secret ever. See if you can find it:

Charm is deceptive, and beauty does not last; but a woman who fears the Lord will be greatly praised. (Proverbs 31:30 NLT)

Do you want to be "greatly praised" for your inner beauty? Then fear the Lord! That doesn't mean that you are supposed to be afraid of God. It's talking about a different kind of fear. It means to think and speak highly of God. Don't use bad words. Never use the Lord's name in vain (saying curse words with "God" or "Jesus" in them). Give God the attention he deserves. Talk to him daily. Thank him for all he has done for you. Read your Bible so you can learn more about him. That's what it means to "fear the Lord."

There will be some very beautiful people who get to heaven and discover that their outer beauty means nothing to God. He will not be impressed. In fact, we won't even have our bodies

> **She knows that the best beauty secret is to see herself through God's eyes.**

in heaven, so outer beauty won't do us any good! There is only one thing God is interested in: our hearts. What do you look like on the inside?

So what about you? Have you discovered the best beauty secret ever? Do you "fear the Lord?"

Well, keep it up, and someday you just might stand before God and hear him say, "Pwiddy gull!" ✻

JUST BETWEEN US

1. Have you ever known someone who is pretty on the outside but not very pretty on the inside? (Don't mention the name—just keep it to yourself!)

2. What do you think Psalm 31:30 means when it says "beauty does not last"?

3. What does the rest of the verse tell us will get praise? What does it mean?

4. What lasts longer: outer beauty or inner beauty?

QUICK BEAUTY TIPS

by Vicki Courtney

YOU'VE PROBABLY HEARD YOUR mom SAY THAT "BEAUTY COMES FROM THE INSIDE" and thought, *Yeah, right Mom—tell other people that.* Well, believe it or not, your mom is right. So, what really makes a girl *beautiful?* Try these beauty secrets:

SMILE: If you haven't discovered this "facelift for free," try smiling more often. It will brighten your entire face.

VOICE: Does your voice sound confident and mature? Some girls carry their "baby talk" voice into their young adult years, and it is not attractive. If you sound like a baby when you talk, chances are, you will be treated like a baby. Let's leave the baby talk for the real babies!

EYE CONTACT: As you speak with people, look into their eyes. When you nervously dart your eyes back and forth, it makes you look shy and insecure.

> Don't feel like you always have to pretend to have your act together.

POSTURE: When I was your age, my mother used to constantly tell me to quit slumping my shoulders and to stand up straight. It drove me crazy . . . until I saw a picture of myself one day and was horrified! My posture made me look so insecure that I started making a concentrated effort to pull my shoulders back and stand taller.

OUTWARD FOCUSED: If a friend has shared a difficulty with you or has expressed sadness over something, do you remember to ask her how she is doing the next time you see her? You can even write her a note, send her an e-mail, or call her to see how she is doing.

ABILITY TO LAUGH AT YOURSELF: Have you learned to laugh at yourself when you do something embarrassing? Each one of us is going to blow it from time to time, whether we trip and fall or say something that doesn't make sense. Rather than act uncomfortable, just crack up! If you don't make a big deal of it, chances are, no one else will either.

ABILITY TO ADMIT WEAKNESSES OR FLAWS: Everyone has weaknesses—it's a fact. Don't feel that you always have to pretend to have your act together. If you make a mistake, just own it and say, "Whoops, I made a mistake." You won't believe how good it feels!

REJOICE WITH THOSE WHO REJOICE: Very few people (including Christians) can really be happy when others around them succeed at something or have something wonderful

> Confidence comes from being sure of yourself and appreciating the gifts God has given you.

happen to them. However, the Bible tells us to "rejoice when others rejoice."

ATTITUDE: Have you noticed how your attitude can affect what happens? Remember, you can always choose your attitude.

COMPASSION: If someone is sad, do you make an effort to speak comforting words to her? A simple "I'm sorry you're going through that. Is there anything I can do to help?" goes a long way and, most importantly, reveals the beauty in your heart.

CONFIDENCE: There is a big difference between being confident and being stuck-up. Confidence comes from being sure of yourself and appreciating the gifts God has given you. Stuck-up is when you have a high opinion of yourself and take credit for the gifts God has given you.

SERVANT'S HEART: I am shocked at the number of people who have never been taught to look out for the needy. I have watched kids and teenagers rudely brush past elderly people—practically knocking them over—when heading through a door. If you see people in need, elderly or not, offer to help them. A servant's heart is one of the most beautiful character qualities there is.

The way you treat your parents, brothers, and/or sisters:

There is nothing more unattractive than a girl snapping sarcastically at her parents or her brothers and sisters in public. If this is a problem for you, learn to hold your tongue, take a deep breath, and talk calmly when the time is right.

Be yourself:

Most girls are so busy trying to be like someone else that they forget the person that God created them to be. Don't be afraid to be you! You are a unique creation of God.

Faith:

A girl who loves Jesus more than life can't help but shine from the inside out. She will brighten every room she enters, and her glow for Christ will be contagious. ✱

Don't be concerned about the outward beauty that depends on fancy hairstyles, expensive jewelry, or beautiful clothes. You should be known for the beauty that comes from within, the unfading beauty of a gentle and quiet spirit, which is so precious to God.
(1 Peter 3:3–4)

RU N2 THe COMPARISON GAME?

by Vicki Courtney

I have the best job in the world. I get to travel to different places and teach girls and moms about God's love. One time, when I was speaking to a group of women, I asked them this question: "If you could be any person in the world, who would you want to be?" I could tell they were thinking about it because I saw them scratching their heads, turning to their friend next to them, and shrugging their shoulders. After a few minutes, I told them that I had brought a framed picture of who I would want to be.

I asked for a few volunteers to come up and take a peek at the picture in the frame and see if it was the same person they had picked. One by one they came up and looked at the picture. One by one, they quickly shook their heads "no."

When the women returned to their seats, I turned the frame around for everyone in the audience to see. It was a mirror! When I look in the mirror, who do I see? Me! I was showing them that if I could choose to be anyone in the world, I would choose to be me.

I felt sad that when the other women looked into my mirror, they said they wouldn't have chosen to be themselves.

Would you choose to be yourself if you could choose to be anyone in the world? You may have said yes right away, but I bet there have been times you have wanted to be like someone else. Maybe someone you watch on TV? Or maybe the pretty girl in class? Or maybe the one who always gets picked first in gym?

We have all compared ourselves to someone else and wished for a minute that we were them. I'm going to let you in on a little secret. The truth is, many of us moms deal with the same thing. I call it the "if only" disease. You know, that's the disease you get when you

WOULD YOU CHOOSE TO BE YOUR-SELF IF YOU COULD CHOOSE TO BE ANYONE IN THE WORLD?

say to yourself, "If only I had her _____" (fill in the blank). Here are some common things you might write in that blank:

CUTE
PERSONALITY

MONEY

COOL
CLOTHES

FRIENDS

FAMILY

ATHLETIC
ABILITY

GOOD GRADES

COOL STUFF

TALENT

HAIR

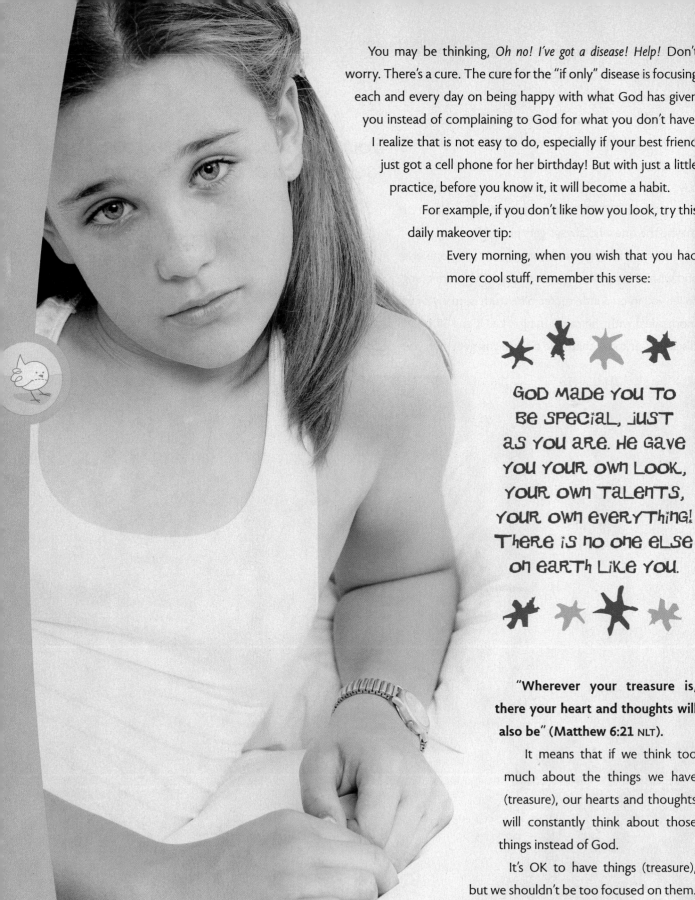

You may be thinking, *Oh no! I've got a disease! Help!* Don't worry. There's a cure. The cure for the "if only" disease is focusing each and every day on being happy with what God has given you instead of complaining to God for what you don't have. I realize that is not easy to do, especially if your best friend just got a cell phone for her birthday! But with just a little practice, before you know it, it will become a habit.

For example, if you don't like how you look, try this daily makeover tip:

Every morning, when you wish that you had more cool stuff, remember this verse:

GOD MADE YOU TO BE SPECIAL, JUST AS YOU ARE. HE GAVE YOU YOUR OWN LOOK, YOUR OWN TALENTS, YOUR OWN EVERYTHING! THERE IS NO ONE ELSE ON EARTH LIKE YOU.

"Wherever your treasure is, there your heart and thoughts will also be" (Matthew 6:21 NLT).

It means that if we think too much about the things we have (treasure), our hearts and thoughts will constantly think about those things instead of God.

It's OK to have things (treasure), but we shouldn't be too focused on them. Sometimes when I find myself wishing I looked like someone else or had someone else's money, talent, or stuff, I stop and say "thank you" to God for what I *do* have. If you begin to thank God for his blessings instead of complaining to him (or your mom!), before long thanking God will become easy. You won't even have to think about it.

God made you to be special, just as you are. He gave you your own look, your own talents, your own everything! There is no one else on earth like you. So, what do you say? If you could be anyone in the world, would you choose you? I sure hope so!✳

JUST BETWEEN US

1. If someone had asked you the same question I asked the women in my group, who would you have said you wanted to be? (Be honest!)

2. Why would you want to be the person above?

3. Why do you think it's so hard for girls and women to be happy with being the person God created them to be?

4. Stop and say a short prayer and tell God "thank you" for creating you to be unique and special. Say it like you mean it!

AidyN

What Makes a Girl?

START

by Susie Davis

I hate pink.

I think frogs and snakes are cool.

✓ I like to watch football with my dad.

I like pink.

Soccer is the sport for me.

My room is decorated with posters of my favorite sports heroes.

Frogs and snakes are slimy and gross.

I really like to wear twirly skirts and sparkly sandals.

Painting my toenails is a must.

Dance is the sport for me.

My room is decorated with posters of my favorite celebrities.

I can't wait to wear makeup.

If I am going skiing in the mountains, I'm concerned about finding a really cute ski outfit.

✓ I like to go shopping with my mom.

I think about boys (and having a boy-friend) all the time.

My idea of a great vacation is going to the largest mall in America!

My ideal movie is about a girl and a boy falling in love.

I don't want to get my hair yucky and wet playing in the rain.

If only I could learn to flat iron my hair by myself.

My idea of a great vacation is going camping and sleeping in a tent!

If I am going skiing in the mountains, I'm concerned about learning how to ski well.

If only I could learn to shoot a BB gun by myself.

My ideal movie is an adventurous story with loads of action.

I really like to wear jeans and a T-shirt.

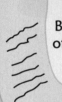

I don't care about makeup at all.

Playing outside in the rain (and getting kind of muddy) sounds really fun.

I wouldn't dream of painting my toenails.

Boys are not on my list of things to think about right now.

If I could, I'd like to play flag football with the boys.

A ponytail works for me.

I love styling my hair.

If I could, I'd like to go to Cotillion and dance with the boys.

...the Truth!

You are a girl whether you like pink or not! Being a girl is not just about what kind of clothes you wear or what you like to do on the weekends. It's not just about whether you want to paint your toenails or wear lip gloss. Girls are all different. Just look around you. Some girls like to watch football with their dads, and some girls like to go shopping with their moms—but no matter which, *they are all girls just the same.*

The fact is, *being a girl is something God designed you to be* when he created you. Psalm 139:13 says, "For you created my inmost being; you knit me together in my mother's womb" (NIV). God made you a girl in your mother's womb. There was nothing that you did or didn't do to get created that way. God decided. And that's why in the hospital when you were born, the first thing the doctor said to your parents was, "It's a GIRL!" A wonderful girl!✻

Dressed to Lure or be Pure?

by Vicki Courtney

Have you ever been fishing? I have two sons who are crazy about fishing. We live in a neighborhood surrounded by woods, and my boys have discovered that the best part of these woods is the fishing pond hidden away behind our house. I cannot count the number of times they have left the house, fishing gear in hand, in hopes of catching a fish at our neighborhood pond. They take nets, poles, extra line, tackle boxes, and anything they can find in the fridge that a fish might want to munch on.

When they head to the pond, their one goal is to catch a big-mouth bass. Fortunately, my boys are only interested in the challenge of catching them; and once they do, they pull out the hook and throw them right back in for a second chance. (That's your cue to say "Awww, poor little fishies.")

Now, if my sons go to the pond without their gear, do you think they will have any luck catching fish? Not likely. My sons insist that the only reason they are able to snag a big-mouth bass is because of the lure they use. You've seen lures before—they come in all shapes and sizes. Most are shiny and shimmery so the fish will be drawn to them when they see them in the water. Fish wouldn't be interested in a plain ole' hook, now would they? No!

Believe it or not, sometimes the clothes girls wear can act as a lure. Some clothes can catch the attention of others but not in a good way. Dressing to lure means dressing to attract the wrong kind of attention. I'm talking about really tight shirts, short shorts and short skirts, and low jeans with your belly showing. Maybe you've seen girls at your school dress this way. Or maybe you've seen older girls on television dressed this way. I'm pretty sure you have because it's hard to escape them. They are everywhere!

As you get older and your body changes, you will realize that there are a lot of fashions sold in stores that could act as a lure: the kind of clothes that attract the wrong kind of attention. To be clear, I'm not talking about clothes that are a fun style or bright colors. I'm talking about clothes that God would not approve of and want you to wear. Sadly, a lot of girls don't realize that what they wear can be a reflection of who they are on the inside. When you believe in Jesus Christ, he comes to live inside you. You know the song, "This Little Light of Mine, I'm Gonna Let It Shine"? Well, when you dress to lure, you draw the attention away from God and put it on yourself. Your light for Christ has a hard time shining through for others to see if everyone is looking at you instead.

Christian girls should dress to be pure. Dressing to be pure means wearing clothes that God would approve. In 1 Corinthians 6:19–20, God tells us that our bodies are not our own, we were bought at a price, and therefore, we should honor God with our bodies! Dressing to be pure shows that you feel good enough about yourself and don't need to "lure" the wrong kind of attention. A good exercise to do is what I call a "mirror check." A mirror check is when you stand in front of a mirror each morning and say, "Would Jesus want me to wear this outfit?" That's basically what it means to honor God with your body like the Bible verses above talked about.

I know it may be hard to see all the fashions and want to fit in with some of the other girls who are wearing clothes that "lure." I am not saying you can't be in style. It is possible to dress in a way that is both fashionable and pure, but it will take extra time and patience to find clothes that would pass the mirror test. As a homework assignment (don't worry—you won't be graded!), you might want to take a look in your closet just to make sure your clothes say "pure" instead of "lure." If they say "lure," it might be time to go "fishing" for a new wardrobe! ✱

JUST BETWEEN US

1. **Have you seen girls dressed in a way that says "lure" instead of "pure"?**

2. **Do you think it's possible to find stylish yet pure clothes?**

3. **Do the clothes in your closet mostly say "lure" or "pure"?**

HOW TO STAY IN LINE ONLINE

WHEN YOU'RE

by Vicki Courtney

I know it's hard for girls today to realize what life was like before there were computers. Back in my day we had to go to the library to look things up. And if someone wanted to talk to us, they had to call the home number. If you were really lucky, you had your own phone line and a phone in your room. There was no such thing as a cell phone, so forget about being able to reach someone whenever you wanted. I remember the frustration of trying to reach a friend and hearing a busy signal. Because there was no such thing as call waiting, we had to keep trying until the line was clear. (Some of my friends were brave enough to do an "emergency breakthrough," where you call the operator and give her the number you are trying to reach. The operator asks your name and then breaks into the line and announces that there is an "emergency call" and gives your name. I was always too afraid to try it because I heard that sometime he operator would stay on the line to see if it was really an emergency.) Today, if you want to reach someone, you have many options. Some of you may already have cell phones or be able to use Instant Messenger (IM) or e-mail on the computer. If you're not allowed yet, don't worry about it! You're not alone—I promise! It won't be long before your parents allow you to do some of these things . . . and when they do, I want you to be prepared for it.

When it comes to computers, it's a good idea to have some rules to keep you safe. When you go on the Internet, you can connect with the World Wide Web. That's what the "www" stands for. And get this: More than 990,000,000 people in the world go on the Internet. They may not all go on at the same time, but that's how many people use the Internet! Have you ever wondered how many pages are on the Internet? There are more than 4 billion pages, and about 10 million new pages are added each day! I don't think we'll see any world records where someone reads every page on the Internet, do you? And besides, it wouldn't be a good idea to even try because a lot of the pages are bad sites—sites that you should not see, even when you are an adult. The problem is that sometimes kids your age will acciden-tally click on some-thing and go to one of these bad sites. Or maybe it even pops up in a window on your computer. Or some kids click through on a link someone sends them. Some are curious and try to find bad sites on purpose. I wish I could tell you that there is a way to live your entire life without ever seeing one of these bad sites, but chances are you will stumble upon one sooner or later. So, what can you do to keep from seeing these bad sites and stay safe when you're on the computer?

Here are 5 tips to remember when you go on the Internet:

1. If you are allowed to go on the Internet for school assignments, be careful when doing Google searches. Sometimes links to bad sites can come up, so read the information carefully before clicking through to a site.

2. Never talk to strangers online. If some-one you don't know tries to talk to you online, tell your parents immediately.

3. Do not surf around on blogging sites such as Xanga and MySpace. There is a lot of bad stuff on these sites, and it is easy to stumble onto things that can rob you of your innocence.

4. You are too young to have a MySpace page (or one like it on another blog-ging site). The minimum age is usually fourteen or higher so kids your age have to lie about their age to break the rules (which, last I checked, is WRONG!).

5. If you acci-dentally end up on a bad site, click out of it as fast as you can or scream for your mom or dad to come help. Sometimes curiosity makes it hard not to look, but don't do it. What you see can stay in your mind for a long time.✳

THE PROBLEM IS THAT SOMETIMES KIDS YOUR AGE WILL ACCIDENTALLY CLICK ON SOMETHING AND GO TO ONE OF THESE BAD SITES.

IM: **__tishaKat___**

Webcam   Invite

Kat___**: Hey girlfriend!

_chick: wot UP? GBH GBH!

_haKat___**: I've not heard from U in 4EVER! Did you curl up
_?????

_chick: BIOYN!!! U know where I've been...

Kat___**: XUM!!!!!!!!! LOL

So have you heard from M?

_haKat___**: NOPE, not a peep. Guess I'm 2 good

_692__chick: JM2C, but he's a jerk... BTHOOM why he doesn't call.

_tishaKat___**: I'll see him tomorrow in History. Maybe
_'s 4gotten all about me! >:X

_1692__chick: <:-O AYSOS??? get a grip! that will NEVER happen!

_tishaKat___**: WEG... Got to go, I've got POS...

_1692__chick: CUL, LYLAS!

*__tishaKat___**: XOXOXO

B I U [   ] ○

Send

IM (Instant Messaging) Rules:

by Vicki Courtney

Some girls your age are allowed to IM, and some are not. If you're not, don't feel left out—I promise you are not alone! There's plenty of time for it when you are older.

My kids weren't allowed to IM at your age, and at the time they weren't real happy about it. Now they are older and allowed to IM but not without some rules. If or when you are allowed to IM, here are some smart rules to live by:

IM Rules to Live By

Send File   Webcam   Invite

1. Try to get in the habit of asking yourself on a regular basis, "Would what I am typing bring glory and honor to God?" Would it make him smile?

2. If you have a profile, would someone who reads it figure out that you are a Christian after reading it? If the answer is no, why not?

3. Do people share gossip with you online? If so, don't feel special—they gossip with you because they know you will listen to it, and that's not a good thing!

4. Be careful when clicking through to links on other people's profiles. Many lead to bad sites, and some can even give your computer a virus.

5. Always imagine that what you are about to type could be copied and pasted by the other person and used against you in the future. If what you are going to say is not something you are comfortable with others reading, don't type it.

6. Never talk to strangers online, and to be safe, never list your last name, school, phone numbers, or any other personal information in your profile or away message.

7. If your friends use bad language, be brave and tell them to clean it up. If they keep using it, block them.

8. Make sure your screen name would make God proud. I was shocked that one of my daughter's friends from summer camp had a screen name that partly read "Christianhottie"!

9. Remember that e-mail and IM messages are often misunderstood. Save your serious conversations for the phone or, better yet, face-to-face.

10. Always remember that many parents have a program installed on their home computers that can track every IM conversation, every e-mail sent or received, every keystroke typed, and every Web site visited, and then send copies of it to the parent's e-mail address. Whenever you e-mail, IM, or send a text message to someone, there's a good chance that his or her parents can see everything you type. Most importantly, God sees it!

11. If someone you don't know tries to talk to you online, tell your parents. This also goes for someone you do know who threatens you or says anything that makes you feel uncomfortable.

12. Don't spend all your time IMing. When possible, it's always better to talk to friends face-to-face!

13. Last but not least, live by Philippians 4:8, which says, "Finally, brothers, whatever is true, whatever is noble, whatever is right, whatever is pure, whatever is lovely, whatever is admirable—if anything is excellent or praiseworthy—think about such things" (NIV). ✻

CHEATING: The Real Story

by Whitney Prosperi

It started small. Alicia had forgotten to study for the quiz, so when she took a peek at her neighbor's paper, she felt relieved when she saw the right answer. A few minutes later she looked again. Her teacher didn't seem to notice, and besides, it seemed like everyone in her class cheated. That's how cheating became a part of her life. It was so easy at first, and then it seemed like she thought of all kinds of ways to make good grades the "easy way." Alicia was sure she had everyone fooled from her parents to her teachers. But there was someone who wasn't fooled—God. He saw it all. And he wasn't pleased.

Numbers 32:23 says, "Be sure your sin will catch up with you" (HCSB). Can you believe that this is the first Bible verse my mom taught me when I was little? And you know what? I found out that it is true. When we choose to sin, even when we think no one knows, at some point the truth will come out. That's just the way it is. We may go for awhile without anyone knowing, but eventually we'll be found out.

If you cheat on a test, even though you think you got away with it, you didn't. God knows. If you share answers with someone from your homework, you may think no one knows, but God does. And he not only knows, but he cares. He takes cheating seriously. **When we cheat, we're really cheating against him.** That's the way all sin is. Sin goes against God.

As Christians we're supposed to do the work that's assigned to us as if we're working for God. Have you ever thought about that before? When you write your book report, it's not really for your teacher. It's for God. When you're working on that group project, you're not turning it in so your group gets a good grade; you're working for him. He wants us to do the work put in front of us in a way that honors him.

How can you do your schoolwork so that it pleases God? **Maybe you have fallen into some habits of cheating that you need to break.** If so, talk to a parent or youth leader. You may want to ask them to help you make a plan to stop cheating. You may need to go to a teacher and tell her what you've done. Prepare yourself for how she'll handle the situation. She may want you to redo some work, or she may lower your grade on the assignments you cheated on. If you need to ask your teacher to change your seat in her class, then do that. Do whatever it takes to stop cheating. **You may think you're getting away with it**, **but remember, you're not. God sees and wants you to get help. Will you take the first step today?**✱

> **WE MAY GO FOR AWHILE WITHOUT ANYONE KNOWING, BUT EVENTUALLY WE'LL BE FOUND OUT.**

JUST BETWEEN US

1. Have you ever cheated before? (Be honest—no one is grading this paper!)

2. If you have cheated, did you feel badly about it at the time? What about now?

3. Do you think that cheating makes you feel closer to God or further apart from him?

4. If you have cheated before and you are truly sorry, tell God about it and ask for forgiveness. (Don't worry—he knows already!)

Quiz

COPY CAT

by Susie Davi

There's nothing more frustrating than a friend who copies everything you do! And while that is totally irritating, sometimes we can get into the trap of being a copy cat ourselves. Take this quick quiz to see if you are a COPY CAT!

1. One of your friends comes to school and you just love the new jeans she is wearing. Do you:

A) Compliment her and go on your way.

B) Ignore the fact that she has new jeans because you're jealous.

C) Ask her where she got them—so you can go get a pair just like them.

2. A teammate decided to get bangs cut for the first time. She asked everyone she knew if she should try it, and she finally got up her courage and did it. Do you:

A) Tell her the bangs look great and give her a hug.

B) Act like you didn't notice she got new bangs.

C) Say, "Well, it's about time!" and then go home, get out a pair of scissors, and cut some bangs on your own hair.

3. You and a bunch of your friends are going out to eat. You're all sitting at the table ready to order. Do you:

A) Look over the menu quickly and pick out what you would like to order and tell the waiter as soon as he pulls out his pad and pen.

B) Order what you think you want but then change your order after a few of your friends order—worried you might not have ordered the best thing.

C) Tell the waiter you want to go last so you can figure out which food item is the most popular with your friends. Then once they all order, you place yours, which is the same as theirs.

4. Your mom decided you need some new clothes because you've grown so much this year. Do you:

A) Make a plan to go out shopping with your mom at the stores she chooses.

B) Throw a fit and tell her it's too boring and stressful to go shopping with her.

C) Take a poll at school, asking all your friends where they buy their clothes and then hand the list to your mom, telling her that the only way you'll go shopping is to go and buy at the stores where your friends buy their clothes.

5. This summer your parents planned for you to go to an overnight camp for the first time. Do you:

A) Get online with your parents and go to the camp Web site. You look at all the photos of the camp and print a copy of the "what to bring" list so you can start getting ready.

B) Roll your eyes and tell them that camp is not your thing.

C) Anxiously grab the phone and start calling every friend you know to see if they can talk their parents into letting them go to camp with you.

6. Your parents decided that your family is going to start going to church every Sunday. Do you:

A) Tell them you are excited about the idea of meeting new friends that believe in God.

B) Warn them that you really have no plan for getting up early on Sunday and going to church.

C) Tell your parents you'll only go where your friends go, so they should probably start calling your friends' parents.

MoSTLy "A" You're the DAWG! You are able to make decisions by yourself and able to stand on your own, which allows you to experience all life has for you! You have strong confidence in the marvelous way God made you. Way to go!

moSTLy "B" OK—so you could use an adjustment in your attitude about new things and standing alone. Life is full of great surprises, and the truth is, you're missing out by not being more open-minded. In addition, your ungrateful attitude is likely to make people dislike being around you. Try to be more flexible and positive!

MoSTLy "C" Meow! You're a COPY CAT! Your decisions are ruled by what others think of you. While it is important to enjoy your friends, you are too controlled by what they think and do. Why not pray for courage to make some good decisions all by yourself, whether that is what you will wear to school or which camp you go to this summer. You are created by God, and he thinks you are fabulously made—and that includes your ideas about what you think is pretty or what your favorite food may be. Celebrate the unique you! ✳

DO YOU FIT In?

by Vicki Courtney

Not long ago I went to a meeting at my son's high school where there were about three hundred students gathered together. The reason for the meeting was to have a vote on the theme for the homecoming dance. Now you probably haven't had any dances at your school, but when you get older, you'll see what I'm talking about. The homecoming dance is the most important dance all school year, so they give it a decorating "theme." Maybe your bedroom has a theme, like butterflies or flowers. I have a two-year-old niece, and she is obsessed with Dora the Explorer, so you can guess what the theme is in her bedroom! At this meeting the students were given four choices for the theme (don't worry—Dora was *not* one of them!). They were then asked to raise

their hands when their favorite theme was called. I noticed a group of about ten girls whispering back and forth about which theme they would vote on. When it came time for the vote and their choice was called, they all confidently raised their hands together. They were sure this was the theme they wanted. As soon as their hands went in the air, they glanced around the room. Out of three hundred people, only a few other people had picked that theme. Their choice was not the popular choice. A few of the girls became really uncomfortable and quickly lowered their hands before their vote was counted. They wanted so badly to fit in that they changed their vote just to go along with the crowd!

Almost every child, tween, teen, and even adult wants to fit in. Sooner or later, you will be

faced with a time where you will have to choose to "fit in" with the crowd or "stand strong" for what you believe in. Standing strong may be hard—and may even mean that you won't be popular. As a Christian, this can be a real tough challenge if "fitting in" means going against your faith or belief in God. Believe it or not, the Bible talks about three teenagers in the Bible who had to face that very challenge! And get this—standing strong cost them much more than just popularity—they almost lost their very lives.

Maybe you remember the story of Shadrach, Meshach, and Abednego. You may have even seen the VeggieTales version of the story with Rack, Shack, and Benny in the chocolate factory! Remember the song? "The bunny, the bunny, oooh, I love the bunny...." OK, before you get that song stuck in your head, let's get back to the real story! God told the boys not to worship any gods (or idols) except for him, the one true God. The king at the time, King Nebuchadnezzar, didn't believe in God, and he gave a command for all the people in the land to fall down and worship a gold statue (idol) he had created. (Sorry VeggieTales fans—it was not really a chocolate bunny!) Now, this was not your

ALMOST EVERY CHILD, TWEEN, TEEN, AND EVEN ADULT WANTS TO FIT IN.

average gold statue. It was ninety feet high! That's about fifteen people your dad's height standing on each other's shoulders! The king told everyone that they should bow down to this gold statue whenever they heard the sound of the horn, flute, harp, and all kinds of music. In other words, when the music started playing, hit the dirt! **Then the king said that anyone who refused to fall down and worship the gold image would immediately be thrown into a blazing furnace!** Have you ever been to a camp out and felt the heat coming from the campfire? Well, this is like thousands and thousands of campfires in a giant metal fireplace. And believe me, the king wasn't planning to use it to roast marshmallows!

They Refused To Bow Down and Worship The Golden image.

When the music began playing, you can bet that everyone hit the dirt—everyone that is, except Shadrach, Meshach, and Abednego. They refused to bow down and worship the golden image. Someone told the king, and he asked to see the boys. (Don't you hate tattletales?!) The king gave them one more chance to bow down and worship the golden image and reminded them that if they didn't, they would be tossed into the fiery furnace.

Now stop for a minute and think about their situation. **It is normal to want to go along with what everyone else does.** And it is even more normal to WANT TO LIVE! Yet these boys overcame the temptation to follow the crowd and bow down to the image. Remember the girls voting on the homecoming theme? **They felt out of place with just three hundred other students.** Picture a much, much larger group of people, and try to imagine these three boys standing while everyone else is bowing down. Would you have continued standing the first time the music played? I hope so.

OK, now let's fast-forward to when the king decides to give them one more chance to bow down and worship the golden image. Now what would you do? Would you still be standing when the music began to play again? That's a tough decision, isn't it? Let's check back in on our boys Shadrach, Meshach, and Abednego and see what they decided to do. The Bible tells us that this is what they told the king:

"Nebuchadnezzar, we don't need to give you an answer to this question. If the God we serve exists, then He can rescue us from the furnace of blazing fire, and He can rescue us from the power of you, the king. But even if He does not rescue us, we want you as king to know that we will not serve your gods or worship the gold statue you set up" (Daniel 3:15–18).

Wow! Forget the music and send the orchestra home. No need even to play a note; these boys had made up their minds. **They knew their God *could* rescue them, but they did not know whether he actually *would* rescue them. They were willing to stand up for God, even if it meant they could die.** Most of us, even if we had made it through the first song still standing, would have probably bowed down the second time after one look at that fiery furnace. So what do you think happened to the boys? There is bad news and good news. Let's start with the bad news. The Bible tells us the king was so angry that he had the furnace heated up seven times hotter than before! It was so hot that the flames coming up killed the soldiers who brought Shadrach, Meshach, and Abednego over to the furnace! But wait—it gets even worse. True to his promise, the king had the boys thrown into the fiery furnace.

But here's the good news—**when the boys were brought out of the fiery furnace, they weren't harmed at all! Not even a sun-burn on those boys!** And that's not all. Remember how the king didn't believe in God and worshipped that stupid ninety-foot golden statue? When the boys came out of the fire, the king knew that only the one true God could have saved them, so he made a new law that anyone who ever said anything bad about the boys' God would be cut into pieces!

In the same way, we should care more about serving God than bowing down to the things around us. Now I don't imagine you will be asked to bow down to a ninety-foot golden statue any time soon (or ever!), but there are plenty of other things Christian girls will be tempted to do on a daily basis. What about gossip, lying, or disobeying? How about wearing clothes that aren't pure? What about letting a friend copy your homework? Or saying bad words? Or even viewing things on television, the computer, or in the movies that you know your parents don't approve of? **When it comes to the temptation to "fit in," let's try to remember Shadrach, Meshach, and Abednego and how they chose to stand up for God. If they can do it, we can too!** ✳

JUST BETWEEN US

1. Have you ever done something just to fit in? If so, what was it?

2. Do you think you would have been more like Shadrach, Meshach, and Abednego who stood up for God, or like the rest of the Israelite boys who just wanted to fit in?

3. Why do some girls want to fit in so badly, even if it means joining the wrong crowd and making bad choices?

4. What sort of things do girls your age "bow down" to (gossip, cussing, cheating)?

Never Ever

Never Ever think you're ugly.

Never Ever believe you can't change for the better.

Never Ever forget that you are wonderfully made.

Never Ever think that you have to look like girls in fashion magazines or TV.

Never Ever talk to anyone online that you don't know.

Never Ever say, "I hate myself."

Never Ever think that your worth is only about your grades at school.

Never Ever believe that your worth is just about how you look.

Never Ever accept the lie that if you aren't "popular" you aren't important.

Never Ever do things that you know are wrong just to be accepted.

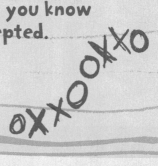

oXXOOXXo

Quiz

aRe You the CENTER of aTTENTION?

by Vicki Courtney

Do you love getting attention? Sure, everybody likes a little attention from time to time, but are you the type that has to have it ALL the time? Take the quiz to find out.

1. A friend calls you and excitedly tells you she is going snow skiing over Spring Break. You went to the same place a few years ago. You . . .

A) let her finish and then tell her that you have been to the same place before.

B) immediately interrupt her and scream, "I've been there!" and then start talking about your trip.

2. You are at gymnastics class, and everyone in your group is talking about how the new girl can do a back flip. You just did it last week, and they weren't there to see it. You . . .

A) join in and agree that her back flip is incredible, knowing they will see yours before class is over.

B) tell them that you did a back flip last week and then show them just to prove it.

3. When you are in a group of friends, you . . .

A) usually let everyone have a turn to talk if they want to.

B) usually do all the talking and often interrupt others when they start talking.

4. You are shopping for new school clothes. When you are trying on an outfit, you find yourself . . .

A) wondering if it is something that looks like "you."

B) wondering if it will impress your friends.

5. You are with a couple of your friends, and they mention a party coming up and ask you if you are invited. You're not. You . . .

A) are pretty sad, but you decide not to make a big deal about it.

B) go on and on to your friends about how no one likes you. You want to make sure they feel sorry for you.

IF YOU ANSWERED "B" TWO OR MORE TIMES, you are trying too hard to be the center of attention. Try to catch yourself when you interrupt others and let them talk. Don't do all the talking and give others a chance to talk. When your feelings get hurt, tell your mom and pray and ask God to comfort you instead of trying to get everyone to feel sorry for you. You may not think it's a big deal to be the center of attention, but after awhile your friends will get tired of it. ✽

they call me "big mouth"

by whitney prosperi

I remember the look on her face when she heard the words come out of my mouth. I didn't mean for her to hear them. I didn't even notice she was standing there. I was with a group of friends and someone mentioned her name. Before I knew it, my big mouth flew open, and I said something very ugly about her. That's when I noticed she was right next to me. And that's when I knew she heard me. The tears filling her eyes told the whole story.

Has anything like this ever happened to you? Maybe you heard someone talk about you, and you know how much that can hurt. You never forgot what she said. Or maybe, like me, your mouth has gotten you into trouble too many times. You have a problem with gossiping about people, talking back to your parents, or saying bad words. If this is you, help is on the way. We'll look at a good cure for our big mouths.

Ephesians 4:29 says, "No rotten talk should come from your mouth, but only what is good for the building up of someone in need, in order to give grace to those who hear." The Bible is pretty clear about what we should and shouldn't say. If it's rotten, we should keep our mouths shut. If it would hurt someone else, clamp it shut. Is it disrespectful? Then put a lock on that big mouth. Think about that for a minute. If we used this verse to decide what to say, how would that change how we talked to our friends and family?

"no rotten talk should come from your mouth, but only what is good for the building up of someone in need, in order to give grace to those who hear."

One good idea for getting our big mouths under control is to memorize the Bible verse above. This isn't as hard as it sounds. Just write out the verse on a little note card or piece of paper and put it on your mirror. When you're getting ready in the morning or brushing your teeth at night, read over the verse. Before you know it, that verse

dorky pathetic gross ugly dumb stupid sissy skanky "did you hear...?" "i hate her" loser fatty will fly off your tongue as fast as all those song lyrics you know. Memorizing is easy. And the great thing is, the more you know God's Word by heart, the more it changes your heart. And the more your heart changes, the more your words change. As a matter of fact, if you want to know what someone is like on the inside, just listen to his or her words. Those give the biggest clues.

One more way to get your mouth under control is to pray about it. Remember that God can do anything—even change our bad habits. So if you know you fall into the big-mouth category, pray everyday that God will help you as you change from a "big mouth" to a "better mouth." He will answer your prayers, but it may take some time, so don't give up. Don't be discouraged if you fall back into an old habit. If you do, quickly ask God to forgive you and ask the person you hurt to forgive you also. Your mouth can change—little by little. Why not start the change today? *

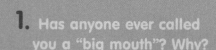

pray every day that God would help you as you change from a "big mouth" to a "better mouth."

JUST BETWEEN US

1. Has anyone ever called you a "big mouth"? Why?

2. Can you think of a time when you got caught spreading gossip? Did you feel bad about it?

3. Say Ephesians 4:29 out loud. Think about writing it down on a note card or maybe your school notebook as a reminder.

4. Can you think of a time when you were hurt by someone else's unkind words? When you think about how it made you feel, does it make you want to watch your own words?

Sweet and Sour

by Vicki Courtney

I own the absolute cutest dog on earth. She is so cute that cars stop and comment on her when I take her for a walk in my neighborhood. She is full grown and weighs a whopping five pounds. She has the face of a bear cub, and her fur is soft as silky cotton. One look and she would melt your heart.

And get this: she even loves to wear clothes! She has a sweater, a pair of pajamas, and a pink T-shirt with "Drama Queen" written on it. Sometimes she will find her shirt in the laundry pile, pick it up with her teeth, and bring it to me to put on her. Who wouldn't want a dog like that?!

When my family decided to buy a puppy a few years ago, I read about all the different types of dogs before we bought her. I knew I wanted a dog that was small, wouldn't shed fur all over the house, and had a great personality. I chose the Yorkshire terrier breed because it matched all the things I was looking for. I found a person who had a "Yorkie" who was expecting puppies, and he put my name on a list. When the puppies were born, he called me to come over and pick out my puppy. **The minute I saw little Lexie, I knew she was meant to be mine.** She didn't even weigh a pound when we got her!

Now my Lexie is full grown, and she is everything that I wanted—she is small, she doesn't shed fur, and she has a great personality. In fact, now that I think about it, she has more than one personality. She goes by a variety of

She goes by a variety of names in our home: Psycho Pup, Devil Dog, and Lucy . . . short for Lucifer!

names in our home: Psycho Pup, Devil Dog, and Lucy (short for Lucifer—another name for the devil). One minute she can be the sweetest, most charming puppy on earth; and the next minute, she can turn into a ferocious beast. **In fact, I often joke that we didn't get a Yorkshire terrier—we got a Yorkshire "terror."**

There have been times when she has chased after my teenage son, growling loudly with her teeth showing, and sent him running in fear of his life. My son is nearly six feet tall, so it's pretty funny to watch. Imagine what a sight it is when I find him standing on the sofa screaming for help at the top of his lungs while this five-pound fur ball with an angelic face and pink hair bow sits at the base of the sofa with her teeth bared just waiting for a piece of him. But minutes later she goes back to being "sweet Lexie" and wags her tail and rolls over to get her tummy rubbed. She will then smother you with wet dog kisses, and you will wonder how you could have ever been afraid of something so sweet and harmless.

Talk about moody! Have you ever felt that way? One minute you're in a great mood, and then all of a sudden, you feel like biting someone's head off—like your mom, dad, or annoying brother. As your body goes through many changes, it can cause you to go up and down with your emotions. One minute you can be laughing, full of life, and social; and the next minute you can be in tears, worn out, and wanting to be alone. Can you relate? If so, you need to know that this is perfectly normal. However, that doesn't mean you can get away with acting like a

Talk about MOODY! Have you ever felt that way?

ferocious beast. Here are some things to remember the next time you are feeling moody.

—Avoid making sudden decisions during this time. When you are emotional, you can sometimes make a bigger deal out of things than necessary. Take a deep breath and pray about it.

—Have at least one person you can talk to. It's great if you can go to your mother and tell her what you are feeling.

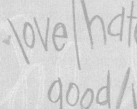

love/hate

good/bad

yes/no

joy/sadness

—When you are moody, try writing your thoughts down in a journal.

—Lean on Jesus Christ. The cool thing about Christianity is that Jesus wants to have a personal relationship with each one of us. He wants us to come to him and share our hurts, fears, and joys.

If you are like most girls, your moodiness should die down as you get older and your body finishes the development process. In the meantime, try not to be as vicious as my Lexie and send everyone running away in fear!

Trust in the LORD with all your heart; do not depend on your own understanding. Seek his will in all you do, and he will direct your paths. (Proverbs 3:5–6) ✻

JUST BETWEEN US

1. Have you ever felt "moody"? Did you tell your mom or talk about it with anyone?

2. Did you know that when your body is going through changes, it can cause your emotions to go up and down?

3. Next time you are feeling moody, tell someone. Can you think of someone right now who would be a good person to talk to?

4. Don't forget to talk to God the next time you are feeling down. Remember, he created you and knows you better than anyone!

Quiz

aRe You RuDe?

by Vicki Courtney

The Bible tells us to "show respect for everyone. Love your Christian brothers and sisters" (1 Peter 2:17a NLT). Do you show respect for everyone, or are you rude and disrespectful? Take the quiz to find out.

1. You walk into a store with your mom just as an elderly woman is walking out. You . . .

A) hold the door open for her as she goes through.

B) let her get the door herself. You're in a hurry—we're talking the mall, right?!

2. Your mother calls to you from another room. You can't hear her very well so you . . .

A) come closer and yell back, "Ma'am?"

B) scream back, "I can't hear you! What do you want?!"

3. Your grandmother calls you to wish you happy birthday. She asks you a bunch of questions about your day. You . . .

A) tell her all about it and thank her for the birthday money she sent you.

B) answer "yeah" to all her questions. You can't wait to get off the phone and get back to your new DVD player.

4. Your mom let you have a friend spend the night and go to your church the next morning. Your pastor preaches a little longer than normal, and you begin to squirm. You . . .

A) try very hard to concentrate on what he is saying.

B) begin passing notes to your friend and giggling. It's just too hard to concentrate.

5. Your mom makes cinnamon rolls one morning for breakfast. You and your sister (or brother) rush to the table. You spot the one you want, and it's the most ooey-gooey cinnamon roll on the plate. You . . .

A) politely ask if you can have it.

B) grab it fast. You're pretty sure you even heard it calling your name.

Total up your answers. How many "A's" did you have? How many "B's" did you have?

IF YOU HAVE 5 A'S: You are a polite, respectful young lady. Keep up the good work!

IF YOU HAVE 3 TO 4 A'S: You are average and there's room for improvement. You're off to a good start. Look for ways that you can show more respect for others.

IF YOU HAVE 1 TO 2 A'S: You need to do a manners check. Chances are, others have noticed that you can be rude, disrespectful, and impolite at times. Pray and ask God to help you show more respect to others. ✳

YOU'RE NOT INVITED

by Susie Davis

Every Valentine's Day is the same. Either you bring a valentine for everyone in your class or not at all. Those are the rules at our school, and those rules are in place so people don't get their feelings hurt from being left out. Those rules also count when it comes to invitations to birth-

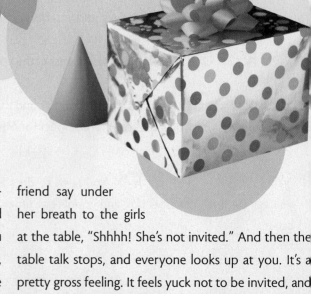

day parties—either you bring an invitation to everyone in the class or not at all. But what about outside of school? The same rules don't apply. There are invitations flying right and left for all those birthday parties your classmates have throughout the school year. Sometimes you are invited and sometimes you're not. And the truth is that even if you aren't good friends with the girl who is having the party, it still hurts when you hear about a party and you're not invited.

It happens something like this. You're in the cafeteria at school, and you just got your tray of food. As you head toward the table where all your friends are sitting, from a distance you can see they all seem to be laughing and having fun. But just when you get close to the table and start to put your tray down, you hear a friend say under her breath to the girls at the table, "Shhhh! She's not invited." And then the table talk stops, and everyone looks up at you. It's a pretty gross feeling. It feels yuck not to be invited, and it feels worse to have all your friends talking about it.

So what's a girl to do about being left out? I mean, it's going to happen at one time or another to all of us. How do you keep your head up when you feel like someone has kicked you in the stomach by excluding you? How do you go through the day feeling like someone out there doesn't like you enough to include you in the fun? And then what do you do after the party when your friends come back talking about what a great time they had at the party that you weren't invited to?

The thing that usually happens when you have been left out is that your feelings get hurt. And when

your feelings get hurt, you sometimes get angry— angry at the person or people who have hurt your feelings. When that happens, you may want to say ugly things about them or give them a bad look at school, but that's really not the best idea because that creates even more problems. So when the time comes that you find yourself left out, I have a few helpful little things to suggest to you.

 First, understand that the situation hurt your feelings. It is good to go ahead and confess that out loud. Maybe tell your mom or your best friend that not being invited to a party hurts.

 Second, realize that there are millions of reasons why you might not have been included, and those reasons don't have anything to do with whether or not you are a fabulous person. Lots of fabulous people aren't invited to parties! And in this case, you are the fabulous person that wasn't invited. Don't let being left out ruin the way you feel about yourself.

 Third, find something else to do when the party is going on. Don't just sit around thinking about being left out. Instead, create a new plan. Look over the suggestions listed below in "What to Do When You're Not Invited" and pick out a few that you could try.

WHAT TO DO WHEN YOU'RE NOT INVITED

Invite over a new friend and take the chance to get to know someone that you don't know well.

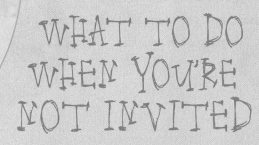

Ask your mom to take you to a local craft store the day of the party and try making something that you have always wanted to try making but never found the time to learn.

Check out a book at the library that you have been dying to read, and make a big bowl of popcorn and jump into a new story.

Gather a few of your neighborhood friends (even if they aren't in your grade) and surprise a few of your neighbors by raking leaves in their yard, or ask permission to wash their cars. Have fun serving someone that lives close by.

Ask your dad or mom on a date. They might even be willing to take you to dinner or to a movie you have been looking forward to seeing.

Call your grandparents and catch up on the phone with them. Or create a homemade card for them and tell them all that is going on in your life.

Last idea—and this might be a hard one to do—make a gift or card for the person who excluded you from the party. Pray and ask God for wisdom to do this, and only do it if you feel you can do it with the right attitude. Sometimes blessing someone who has hurt you (whether she meant to or not) can be the biggest blessing of all back on you.

Fourth, forgive the person who has hurt your feelings. Don't hold a grudge against them. Make sure you don't get into staying angry at the person throwing the party. I found a verse that helps me in this kind of situation; it's Colossians 3:13, and it says, "Put up with each other, and forgive anyone who does you wrong, just as Christ has forgiven you" (CEV). In truth, the person giving the party might not have done anything wrong by not inviting you, but the verse really applies in this case because sometimes we have to put up with each other and forgive.

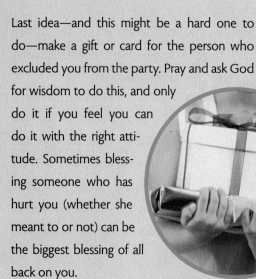

"PUT UP WITH EACH OTHER, AND FOR-
GIVE ANYONE WHO DOES YOU WRONG,
JUST AS CHRIST HAS FORGIVEN YOU."
(COLOSSIANS 3:13)

...nyway—because Christ always forgives us. It's a great
...erse to memorize. And after you get that one tucked
...n your mind, remember to pray and ask God for the
...bility to get over the hurt feelings. He will help you
...ecause he is very interested in being invited in to help
...ou with your everyday life!

JUST BETWEEN US

1. Do you remember a time when you were "not invited"? How did that make you feel?

2. What did you do when you found out that you weren't invited? Was that a good idea or a bad idea? (Was God honored in your actions?)

3. Even if it's not you, there will always be people who don't get invited to certain parties. How can you be more sensitive or thoughtful about parties and invitations in the future?

4. Which one of the "What to Do When You're Not Invited" suggestions would you be mostly likely to try first? Why?

CHAPTER 2: OTHERS

A Girl's Guide

Your friends are some of the most important people in your life. You spend tons of time with them every week. You laugh with them, you play with them, and you share secrets with them. So, because your friends are special people in your life, it's a good idea to know how to get along with them. What better place than the Bible to get some tips on how to be a good friend. Below you will find a girl's guide to friendship—with verses from the Bible to show you how to be a great best friend!

1. Be Selfless: OK, let's be honest—most people think of themselve first. It's natural and it come easy. Whether you are at schoo or playing your favorite sport it's much easier to think abou yourself. But **Philippians 2:4 says "Everyone should look out no only for his own interests, bu also for the interests of others.** This verse tells us to think abou other people, and it reminds u not to be selfish. The opposite o selfishness is selflessness—which is what we should practice wher it comes to our friends. One o my good friends gave me an idea on how to be selfless with others and it's called the "second cookie" tip. It goes something like this

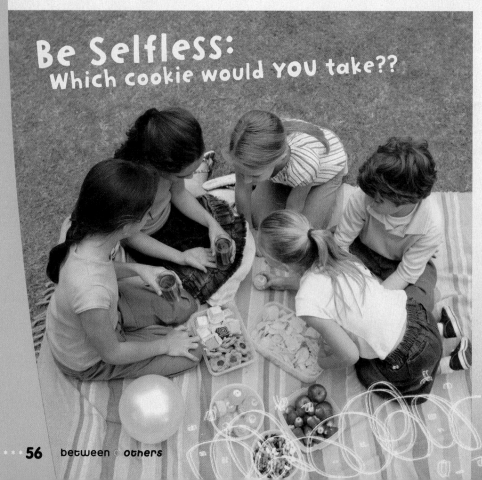

Be Selfless:
Which cookie would YOU take??

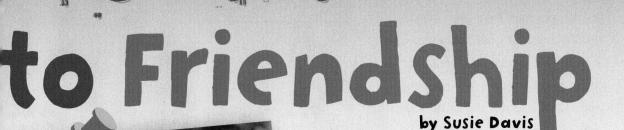

to Friendship

by Susie Davis

or movie instead of you? Or maybe let your friend borrow a book that you were dying to read and were saving for yourself? Whatever comes up with your friend, think of how you can honor her by taking second and going second.

2. Be a Secret Keeper: This should be a no-brainer, especially for girls, but for some reason it is especially hard just to keep our mouths shut when it comes to keeping secrets. **Proverbs 11:13 states: "A gossip goes around revealing a secret, but the trustworthy keeps a confidence."** Do you know what it means to be trustworthy? Being trustworthy means people have confidence in you. And in this case

Let's say that you and your friend are at your house, and your mom has just made her delicious homemade cookies, and they are your absolute favorites. Your mom hands you the plate. . . . What do you do? Do you grab the biggest, most delicious-looking cookie and stuff it in your mouth? Well no, not if you want to be selfless; you let your friends pick first, and you take the "second cookie" or the second-choice cookie, which might be the smaller one. OK, here's another little test. Let's say your friend asks you to take one first; then what do you do? Well, how about choosing the smallest cookie on the plate? That's just one way for you to put others' interests first—you go second or take the second choice. And that works in other areas besides just cookies. What about choosing to let your friend pick a game

Be a Secret Keeper:
Will you keep hers??

it means people have confidence in your ability to keep a secret. Are you trustworthy? If you want good friends, you must be a good friend, and that means you need to be trustworthy. Don't give away secrets that are not yours to give. When a person shares a secret, she trusts you with a little piece of her heart. If you are revealing secrets, you're a gossip, and "a gossip separates friends" (Proverbs 16:28). Decide now that you will be a trustworthy friend.

3. Be Willing to Forgive:
You know the really crazy thing about friends and even best friends? They can let you down. (Even Jesus had friends that let him down.) So it's smart to keep in mind that your friends will hurt your feelings sometimes,

Be a Friend to Many

to you. The Bible says we should overlook it or let it go, and if we do, it will bond, or glue together, a friendship. But if you don't let it go, the Bible predicts that you'll be waving bye-bye to that friend.

4. Be a Friend to Many:
Don't get into the trick of having only one friend. Although it is great to have a best friend, one friend can not and should not meet all of your friendship needs. There is only so much one person can do, and if you lean into your one best friend for every thing, chances are you are going to end up disappointed and frustrated. It's likely that your friend will end up feeling drained and overwhelmed if you are too dependent on her. Instead decide to be a friend to many different people. Enjoy getting to know lots of people in your school or church or neighborhood.

5. Get to Know the Best Friend You'll Ever Have—Jesus:
In the Bible John 15:13 says, "No one has greater love than this, that someone would lay down his life for his friends." Did you know that Jesus did that just for you? He literally laid his life on the line for you so that

Be Willing to Forgive:
Yes, even HER!!

and it is wise to know what the Bible says when we refuse to forgive our friends. Proverbs 17:9 promises: "Overlook an offense and bond a friendship; fasten on to a slight and—good-bye, friend (*The Message*). An offense is when someone does something hurtful you could have eternal life and a relationship with God. You will find no better friend than Jesus Christ. He will never stop loving you. He will never stop caring for you. He will never run out of time for you. Never. As friends in your life come and go, Jesus Christ remains the same yesterday, today, and forever. And because of that promise, you can count on his constant, loving friendship throughout your life. So get to know him well; and as you do, you will find he is the best friend ever. ✽

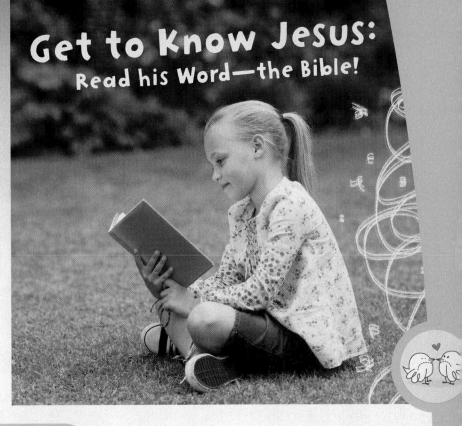

Get to Know Jesus:
Read his Word—the Bible!

JUST BETWEEN US

1. How good are you at being selfless? Think of three ways you can practice putting your friends' interests above your own. Ask God to help you practice selflessness this week.

2. Can you remember a time when gossip hurt a friendship? On a scale of 1 to 10 (1 being not trustworthy and 10 being extremely trustworthy), how trustworthy are you?

3. Is there a friend you need to forgive? What does the Bible say happens when we refuse to forgive a friend?

4. Leaning into only one friend can create problems for a friendship. List five people you would like to get to know better. Now think of creative ways to become friends with those five people. Write down your ideas and share them with your mom or dad to see if they can help you broaden your circle of friends.

5. Get to know Jesus better—your best friend ever. Spend time reading the Bible and praying. Go to church and learn more about him. Hang around people who love Jesus—you will truly find he is the best friend ever!

WANTED: A REAL FRIEND

by Whitney Prosperi

DO YOU REMEMBER A TIME WHEN ONE OF YOUR FRIENDS DIDN'T ACT LIKE A REAL FRIEND? I do. It's a long, crazy story; and trust me, if you could see a videotape of what happened, you would laugh your head off.

One afternoon my friend Tammy and I went to the grocery store to get some snacks. Before we even began our shopping trip, we started goofing around. She is one of those friends who can bring out the fun in everyone, and before long we were speeding through the store with our shopping cart. Before I tell the rest of the story, I should say that this wasn't a good idea, and I wouldn't suggest trying it.

To make a long story short, when Tammy got some speed going, she jumped up on the metal rail under the cart. You probably did this when you were little. So did I. Well, here's a little tip: when you're older, you're too heavy to keep the cart balanced. For this reason the end of the car[t] tipped up, and she fell headfirst into the basket. Nex[t] the shopping cart (with her inside) turned over upside down. It was now completely flipped over and speed[ing] toward the meat counter, which was behind [a] glass case. No kidding!

As you can imagine, most people in the store turned their heads to see a red-head flying by the checkout lines in the basket of an upside-down grocery cart. Honestly, it was one of the funniest things I have ever seen. In case you're wondering about the glass case and my friend's health, she and the meat counter made it just fine. Her hands, which were drug under the weight of the basket (with her in it), were cut and bruised. And of course she was probably more embarrassed than she had ever been before in her entire life.

Now comes the worst part of the story. After Tammy and her racing cart finally stopped and while I was helping her climb out, we noticed one of our other friends a few aisles away staring at us. We knew she had noticed us because at this point everyone in the store had, so we waved at her. And guess what? She acted like she didn't see us and walked the other way. She was ashamed to admit that she knew us.

Ever had a similar experience? I'm not talking about the shopping cart ride or almost crashing into a glass meat counter. I'm wondering if you have ever thought someone was your friend, but when you did something that embarrassed her, she dumped you and turned the other way. We've all been there.

How do you know if you've got a real friend? See if she matches up to what God says about friends in his Word.

> Have ever thought someone was your **friend**, but when you did something that embarrassed her, she **dumped** you and turned the other way?

"A REAL FRIEND STAYS WITH YOU THROUGH GOOD AND BAD TIMES."

1. A real friend stays with you through good and bad times.

A friend loves at all times. (Proverbs 17:17)

Everyone wants to be your friend when things are going well, but what if you do something embarrassing, like trip in the lunchroom? Or what if you do the right thing when everyone else does the wrong one? Will your friend support you, or will she stay silent? True friends stay with you even when it may not be the popular thing to do.

A REAL FRIEND

2. A real friend doesn't repeat what you say.

Whoever conceals an offense promotes love, but whoever gossips about it separates friends. (Proverbs 17:9)

Ever had a friend who couldn't keep her mouth shut? When you would tell her something, she would blab your business to other people. You can trust true friends with the big and small things you tell them. They won't repeat what you've said to others.

"The one who walks with the wise will become wise, but a companion of fools will suffer harm."

(Proverbs 13:20)

3. A real friend makes good choices.

The one who walks with the wise will become wise, but a companion of fools will suffer harm. (Proverbs 13:20)

Real friends help you make good decisions. They don't tempt you to make wrong ones. They don't laugh at you when you want to do what's right; instead, they do the right thing with you. Remember, you will become like your friends—so make sure you choose them carefully.

4. A real friend helps you love Jesus more.

Iron sharpens iron, and one man sharpens another. (Proverbs 27:17)

Real friends encourage each other to follow Jesus. They pray for each other and share what they are learning from God's Word.

What kind of friend are you? Do you stand by your friends even when it would be easy to walk away? Do you keep what they tell you to yourself? Remember, to have a good friend you have to be a good friend. Ask God to help you become a true friend. ✱

JUST BETWEEN US

1. Have you ever had a friend turn her back on you? What happened?

2. Do you have a friend who will stand by you no matter what? Who is it?

3. It's important to have friends who make wise choices. Do you have at least one?

4. After reading the article, do you think you are a "real friend"?

10 Tips on how to SURVIVE MEAN GIRLS...
AND KEEP FROM BECOMING ONE
by VICKi COURTHEY

Let's face it—sometimes girls can be mean. If you don't believe me, just have a sleepover and invite an uneven number of girls. Throw in some popcorn and you've got yourself a show—or better yet, a showdown. Mean girls have always been present through time. They are nothing new. Ask your mom—I bet she can share a story or two about mean girls she knew when she was your age. Even the Bible is chock-full of mean-girl stories. And some of us, if we are honest, would have to admit to being a mean girl from time to time. So, whether you know one or you are one, check out the ten tips that follow:

1} Remember, you are who you hang out with. If you hang out with girls who gossip, talk ugly about others, and leave girls out on purpose, chances are good that you have been dubbed one of the "mean girls" at your school. Choose your friends wisely. If you want to keep from becoming a mean girl, don't hang with girls who have made being mean their favorite hobby.

Do not be misled: "Bad company corrupts good character" (1 Corinthians 15:33 NIV).

2} If you are the victim of a mean girl (the one she's usually mean to), try to avoid her. Don't even give her a minute of your time and energy. Treat her as though she is invisible. Mean girls will usually move on to someone else if they don't get the response they are hoping for.

Blessed is the man who does not walk in the counsel of the wicked or stand in the way of sinners (Psalm 1:1 NIV).

3} I realize that this next one is very hard to do, but the Bible tells us to "pray for those who mistreat you" (Luke 6:28). Very few Christians will succeed in loving their enemies, much less praying for them. The next time someone is mean to you, say a prayer for her. Chances are, she needs it.

Love your enemies, do good to those who hate you, bless those who curse you, pray for those who mistreat you (Luke 6:27–28 NIV).

4} Don't leave other girls out on purpose. Most girls will be drawn to girls they have things in common with. This is normal, and there is nothing wrong with wanting to spend time with some girls more than others. When you were younger, your mom probably made you include all the girls in your class so there were no hurt feelings. As you get older, this becomes harder and harder to do. Try to be kind to everyone. Never close the door to new friendships. You may discover you have things in common with someone who is not in your friend group.

Thus you will walk in the ways of good men and keep to the paths of the righteous (Proverbs 2:20 NIV).

5} If girls like to share gossip with you, don't take it as a compliment. They gossip with you because they know you will probably gossip back. If you tell them that you are not comfortable gossiping about others, it won't take long for your friends to figure out that you are no fun to gossip with. No one wants to gossip with someone who won't play the gossip game. If you don't want to gossip but can't figure out a way to tell your friends, just try being honest by saying: "We shouldn't gossip because it's wrong and I always feel bad after I gossip."

The words of a gossip are like choice morsels; they go down to a man's inmost parts (Proverbs 18:8 NIV).

The tongue has the power of life and death, and those who love it will eat its fruit (Proverbs 18:21 NIV).

6} Remember that anyone who shares gossip with you will also share gossip about you. Never tell a gossip anything you don't want others to know, even if she's a close friend. If you are not getting along with her, what's to keep her from telling your secrets?

If you do have a close friend who is a gossip, you need to gently tell her that gossip is wrong. If she decides to keep it up, you might think about getting a new close friend.

A gossip betrays a confidence, but a trustworthy man keeps a secret (Proverbs 11:13 NIV).

7} A true sign that a girl feels good about herself is when she can be happy for others when they accomplish something. The next time someone gets something that you desperately wanted for yourself, make an effort to be happy with her. If you don't feel like it, act yourself into the feeling. The more you practice rejoicing with others and celebrating their successes, the more of a habit it will become.

Rejoice with those who rejoice; mourn with those who mourn (Romans 12:15 NIV).

8} Remember the general rule: People who make fun of others don't feel good about themselves. They somehow think that if they make fun of others, it will make them look better. Many times the popular girls will be mean because they don't want anyone to take their place. If they want to stay in the popular group, they have to make others look less popular.

Do nothing out of selfish ambition or vain conceit, but in humility consider others better than yourselves (Philippians 2:3 NIV).

9} Don't be a groupie. A groupie is someone who has to be in a certain group of friends. She doesn't want to be friends with anyone who isn't in the group. If the group has a "mean-girl leader," many of the girls in the group will make bad choices just so they can look "cool" and stay in the group. They are too insecure to stand up for what is right. If you are in a group like this, get out! Find new friends.

Hate evil, love good (Amos 5:15a NIV).

10} Find at least one friend who also wants to be a nice girl. Agree to pray for each other. If you can't think of even one friend who is a nice girl and will be a good influence on you, pray and ask God to lead you to one.

Therefore encourage one another and build each other up, just as in fact you are doing (1 Thessalonians 5:11 NIV).✻

Quiz

aRe You a GOOD FRieND?

by Susan Jones

finish these stories to find out!

STORY ONE:

One day you decide you want to go to the _____. Knowing you need Mom's OK, you call out, "MOM,
(place)

can you PLEEEEEEEEEASE take me to the _____." Since your mom is so _____, she, of course, says,
(same place)   *(positive adjective)*

"Sure, honey." Thrilled she said yes, you immediately ask if you can invite _____ to come along. Again,
(name of friend #1)

your mom says "sure." So, you call _____ and her mom agrees to let her go with you. You are both SO
(name of friend #1)

_____ because you've been talking about wanting to go to _____ the whole week!
(expressive adjective)   *(same place)*

Then, out of nowhere, the phone rings and after fighting with your _____ to answer the phone, you
(brother or sister)

learn that the call is for you! "Hi, _____, it's _____. You'll never guess where I'm going! My mom
(your name)   *(name of friend #2)*

is taking me to _____, and I'm allowed to invite one friend! Do you want to go?" You can't
(place nearby you have dreamed about going)

believe it! You've ALWAYS wanted to go there. Then, you remember your conversation with _____.
(name of friend #1)

You respond to _____ and say, "_____."
(name of friend #2)   *(your decision to go with friend #1 or friend #2)*

HOW DID YOUR STORY END? Did you spend the day with friend #1 or friend #2?

IF YOU ANSWERED FRIEND #1, congratulations! You are a good friend. You are faithful and understand the importance of keeping your word. Even if "something better" comes along, you will not ditch a friend.

IF YOU ANSWERED FRIEND #2, you may need to rethink the way you handle friendships. If you were the first friend, how would you feel if she cancelled plans with you to do something else with another friend? Always remember to think of everyone involved when making a decision like this. Sometimes it can be tempting to change your mind if you are given a more fun option. But if you do, your friends may begin to lose their trust in you and what you say you are going to do.

STORY TWO:

School is about to start and you feel _____. Your friend from _____ has just move
(adjective) (place you go every week)

to a new house and now goes to your school! You are _____ because she is really sweet. He
(good adjective)

name is _____.
(girl's name)

Your friends from school, _____, _____, and _____ are the popular girl:
(girl's name) (girl's name) (girl's name)

They aren't really _____, but they don't really want new friends either.
(negative adjective)

At lunchtime on the _____ day of school, you sit with _____. After lunch, you are talkin
(number order like 'first') (name of first girl)

with the popular girls when they say that _____ is _____ _____ and ask you wh
(name of first girl) (expressive adverb) (mean adjective)

you were sitting with her. You don't know whether to agree with them (they are your friends after all), or stick u

for your other friend. After thinking for a second, you _____
(reaction to something mean that was said)

_____.

The next day at lunch, you sit with _____.
(first girl, popular girls, or both)

HOW DID YOUR STORY END?

IF YOU STUCK UP FOR YOUR FRIEND who was new to school, you are a good friend! You are no
tempted to gossip, and you are not afraid to stand up for someone, even if it means your other friends may no
accept you. You understand that it is important to treat everyone with respect. You either chose to sit with he
the next day at lunch, or you arranged for all your friends to sit together!

IF YOU EITHER AGREED WITH THE GIRLS OR DIDN'T SAY ANYTHING, you have som
work to do! Start by looking at the type of friends you have. If your school friends are willing to speak ugly abou
someone else, how do you know they wouldn't someday speak ugly about you? I know it can be hard to do th
right thing, especially if your friends are doing the wrong thing, but a true friend is someone who will stand u
for you. Take opportunities like this to gently remind your friends it is not kind to gossip about others. You ma
have chosen to sit with the popular girls the next day at lunch, but a better choice would have been to either s
with your other friend or invite everyone to sit together. ✳

i give my mom an E for embarrassing

by Vicki Courtney

I remember a time when I was around your age, and my mom was taking my friends and me to the mall. I didn't think it was cool to sit with mom in the front seat, so I sat in the backseat with my friends. Honestly, I was just hoping I could make it the entire car ride without my mom thinking, *Now that's not so bad. She was probably singing to herself, right?* Wrong. She was singing out loud. Really loud. Kind of like when you're in the shower and you don't think anyone is listening. That loud. I sunk down in my seat as my face turned redder than a tomato. I mean, did she think she was auditioning for

"And then it happened. She started singing out loud to the song on the radio."

embarrassing me. Now, don't get me wrong. I love my mom and all, but it just seemed like every time my friends were around, I could almost count on her saying or doing something embarrassing. Well, we had almost made it to the mall and I thought maybe, just maybe, my mom was going to make it without embarrassing me. And then it happened. She started singing out loud to the song on the radio. You may be *American Idol* or something? If I had to give my mom a report card that day, she wouldn't be getting an A, B, or C. I would have given her an **E . . . for embarrassing!**

Does your mom ever say to you, "When you get older, you'll understand?" Or, "You'll appreciate this one day when you have kids." My mom used to say those things to me, and guess what? Now that I'm a mom, I understand. It's amazing how becoming an embarrassing mom can cause you to see things differently about your own embarrassing mom. And get this: someday your children will think you are embarrassing! I know that it's hard for you to imagine that, as cool as you are right now.

Take it from an embarrassing mom—**we don't embarrass you on purpose.** We just can't help it! We are totally and completely in a "grown-up world." And it's probably a good thing. You don't really want a mom who is trying so hard to be in a "kid world" that she dresses like you and your friends, talks like you and your friends, and wants to hang out with you and your friends. Ugh. Talk about embarrassing! Do you know any moms like this? If you could choose between a mom who acted like you and a mom who acted like a mom, I bet you'd pick the second one.

I realize that some of you may have very real reasons to be frustrated when it comes to your mom's embarrassing you. I know mothers who sometimes yell at their daughters in front of other people, tease them about liking a certain boy, criticize them for what they are wearing, and yes, even sing out loud to songs on the radio while driving. But seriously, if your mom embarrasses you a lot, think about sitting down with her and sweetly telling her. Most moms are understanding and can think back to their own childhood years when they had an embarrassing mom.

Leviticus 19:3 (NIV) says: "**Each of you must show respect for your mother and father.**" When your mom embarrasses you, don't speak harshly to her or disrespect her in front of your friends. Wait for the right time to talk with her and politely tell her how her comments or actions made you feel. Chances are, if you treat her with respect, she will treat you with respect in return. Now, does this mean that she'll stop singing those tunes at levels only dogs can hear? Not a chance. ✽

✽ What are some things your mom does that embarrass you?

✽ What is a nice way you could let her know how it makes you feel?

✽ Why shouldn't you say anything to her in front of your friends?

FiveTips to BEING AN AWARD-WINNING DAUGHTER

by Vicki Courtney

Have you ever seen those blue ribbons with "World's Best Mom" or "World's Best Dad" on them? They might be dorky, but I bet your parents would be proud to receive one from you! Being a parent is hard work and, sometimes, a thankless job. As a daughter, you can make Mom and Dad's job easier. Try the five tips on the next couple pages, and who knows . . . your efforts may earn you one of those nifty "World's Best Daughter" blue ribbons to hang proudly in your locker. (Yeah, right!)

1. Show them Respect.

Show them respect. Sometimes it's hard to understand when your parents say and do certain things. **Try not to zone out when your parents start talking, but make an effort to listen carefully to them.** If you don't agree with them, you might have to "agree to disagree." Of course, your parents hold the final say, and you must respect their rules and boundaries. And remember, a simple "yes, ma'am" or "no, sir" can do wonders for your relationship.

Talk to Them. 2.

Talk to them. "How was your day?" "Fine." "Do you have a lot of homework?" "No." "Are you ready for your spelling test tomorrow?" "Sort of." I know it's hard when your parents start grilling you with a bunch of questions, but **look at the positive side: at least they are enough to ask!** Try answering with more than one word. Believe it or not, they are not trying to annoy you; they just want to get into your world. Try sharing something about your day even if they don't start the conversation. Your mom might faint the first time you try it, but trust me—a little effort goes a long way.

3. Say "Thanks" Every Once in a While.

Say "thanks" every once in awhile. Trips to the mall, braces, club teams, summer camp, driving on field trips, baking cookies for the bake sale, emergency runs to the store for poster board for your project, a college education (someday), and the list goes on and on. A parent's job is never done. **Sometimes it's easy to take it for granted and assume parents owe their kids these things. The truth is, there are a lot of kids around the world lacking the bare essentials—a roof over their heads and three meals a day.** Yet many parents are knocking themselves out to shuttle their kids to all their activities, make it to their games, and save enough money to get them some of the stuff on their Christmas wish list. Consider making your parents a thank-you card, or just tell them "Thanks!" every once in awhile.

Give Them a Break. 4.

Give them a break. So Dad mows the lawn in dress socks, loafers, and shorts that are above the knee. Mom can't seem to make it ten minutes without embarrassing you when your friends are over. And bless her heart, the waistband on her jeans comes up to her armpits. As if that's not bad enough, she tucks her shirts in and wears a belt. Yikes! **Most parents are not cool, and it's unreasonable to expect them to be someone they're not.** I know it's hard to believe, but someday you will probably have kids who think you are highly uncool and laugh when they see your old pictures. Have your mom save those super high-waisted jeans for you. You might need them! Ick!

5. Remind Them that They are Loved.

Remind them that they are loved. A few months ago I woke up at 5:00 a.m. to drive to the airport and catch an early flight for an out-of-town speaking engagement. As I was heading down the stairs, I found the greatest surprise from my daughter, Paige. She had taped about ten pieces of notebook paper together and written me a sweet note and draped it across the top of the stairs. I was so touched, I cried. I folded that thing up, put it in my bag, and showed it to all my friends. Other times she will leave me a post-it note on my desk or sneak a note into my bag. I have saved every one of them. **I would rather have her homemade notes than a store-bought gift anyday.** Consider leaving your mom or dad a reminder that they are loved. It can be a simple "I love you" on a post-it note, in an e-mail, or a text message. Guaranteed to make your mom cry . . . or your money back. *

Honor your father and mother—which is the first commandment with a promise—that it may go well with you and that you may have a long life in the land. (Ephesians 6:2—3)

Are You a Good Sister?

by Whitney Prosperi

Have you ever let your brother or sister get in trouble for something you did, even when you knew you should be the one getting punished? I have—and I can't say I'm proud of it. When I was five years old, my younger brother and I were playing in the new house my parents were having built. In order to save money, my mom and dad were doing a lot of the painting themselves. Well, my brother and I were playing in one of the rooms that they had just painted the whitest white you have ever seen. It looked perfect, and we were instructed not to touch the walls or even go near them.

All of that went OK until I wanted to drink a can of orange soda. I should have known better. Those cans always explode and spurt out when you don't want them to—like on a newly painted white wall. Well, you guessed it. I opened it, although it would be more accurate to say that an atomic bomb of orange exploded all over the perfect white walls. What do you think we did? Run to tell our parents so they could clean the walls? Of course not. Instead, we panicked. We ran into

another room and played there until later that night. We acted like nothing happened.

Well, later, when my parents saw the walls, **I wimped out on telling them the truth.** They asked my younger brother what happened, and he told them I spilled the soda. Then they asked me. You guessed it. I lied. I told them he did it. I bet you're thinking, *Wow, I'm sure glad she's not my older sister.* Because I was the oldest, my parents believed that I was telling the truth, and they punished my little brother. I don't think my little brother remembers because he was too young when it happened, but I definitely remember. And it makes me feel sad each time I do.

You probably have your own story of a time when you were mean to a brother or sister. It's so easy to do. They are around ALL the time, so we are tempted to take them for granted.

Maybe your brother or sister is younger and constantly follows you around. Or they might not take good care of your personal stuff. Sometimes it's hard to be nice when they are driving you crazy.

We all know the children's rhyme, "Sticks and stones can break my bones, but words will never hurt me." While that little saying is easy to remember, it really isn't true at all. **Words can hurt more than anything. And girls especially know the thing to say that will hurt the worst.** It's not something to brag about.

How about you? What kinds of words fly out of your mouth when you're talking to your brothers and sisters? Do you regularly tell them they are stupid or scream at them when they do something that bugs you? Do you make fun of them or just plain ignore them? If so, keep in mind that they will always remember the things you said to them. You may need to choose to shut your mouth before it hurts them even more. **Colossians 4:6 says, "Let your conversation be always full of grace, seasoned with salt, so that you may know how to answer everyone"** (NIV).

God put you in your exact family for a reason.

Did you know that God put you in your exact family for a reason? He chose your parents and your brothers and sisters. It is not an accident that they are in your life. Think about it for a minute. **He may want you to help your brother or sister in some way.** You can do this by choosing kind words and forgiving them when they bug you. Or you could listen to them or sometimes include them in your more grown-up activities. The more you choose to be nice to them, the more you'll find that all of a sudden they don't bug you so much. ✳

JUST BETWEEN US

1. **If you have a brother or sister, have you ever blamed them for something they didn't do? What was it?**

2. **What is most annoying about your brother or sister?**

3. **What would they say is most annoying about you?**

4. **Next time you are not getting along with your brother or sister, stop and remember that God put them in your family for a reason. Say a prayer and ask God to help you love them even when they aren't being very lovable.**

Do You Have a 'Tude?

by Susie Davis

Did you know that you can say things without using your words? Or even without using your mouth? There is something very powerful that you use every day to speak to people, and it's called nonverbal communication. *Nonverbal* basically means "without words." *Communication* means "getting information to someone else." So in this case, when you are getting information to someone else without your words, you are communicating nonverbally. A little confused? OK, imagine this.

You are outside having fun playing soccer with your neighborhood friends. You just scored a goal, and your team has taken the lead. Then your mom steps out on your front porch and yells out, "It's time to come inside and get started on your homework." And then you look up and yell back, "Just one more minute, Mom. We're in the middle of a game here!" Then your mom shakes her head and replies, "No, come inside this minute—time for schoolwork." You look up and make a sad face back at her and say, "But Mom, please . . ." Then she straightens her back and puts her hands on her hips, and upon seeing her, you know you are two seconds from getting into trouble, so you roll your eyes and heave a heavy sigh, tossing the ball to your friends as you

ANGRY

slowly slouch your way up to your front porch Then when you get to the front door, you look up at your mom and give your eyes one final rol and give one more deep sigh, your shoulders dipped low. Just then your mom looks you square in the face and says, **"Better watch that attitude, little lady, or you're gonna get yourself into trouble. You've got a 'tude (attitude)!"**

You see, in that story it wasn't the words that were causing the problem; it was the body language or the nonverbal communication. It was the

eye rolling, the sad face, the heavy sigh, the slouchy walk, and the drooping shoulders. All that body action said to your mom, "I'm angry about coming inside, and I want you to know about it!" And likewise, your mom had some things to say nonverbally—when she shook her head, straightened her back, and put her hands on her hips. All that body action of hers said, "I am serious about you obeying me and getting in the house and doing some homework."

Nonverbal communication is very powerful. **Have you ever heard the saying that actions speak louder than words? Well, it's true.** Our body language, or nonverbal communication, is actually more convincing than your words. Scientists that study nonverbal communication say that body language speaks louder because people will believe what they see your body

YOUR ATTITUDE SHOULD BE THE SAME AS THAT OF CHRIST JESUS.

Philippians 2:5

saying *before* they will believe what they hear your words saying.

Try this. Look in a mirror and say, "So nice to meet you." Now say it again, but this time add a feeling on your face when you say it. Try to say it while making a face that looks bored. Next say it with a face that is really happy. OK, now try it with a face that is scared. That's a funny thing to do in the mirror, but you have to admit that the words kind of get lost when you see a face with feelings on it. **The truth is, people are more likely to believe your face than believe your words.** So if you say, "So nice to meet you" but your face shows that you are bored, people are likely to think you aren't so glad to meet them. The reason that happens is because of body language.

Next time you feel that nasty, bad attitude creeping in, just whisper a prayer.

God made us to speak with our words and our bodies, and it's a wonderful thing to be able to do both. But we need to remember we are responsible for both too. When our body language has a bad attitude, we're responsible for that, just as we are responsible for our words.

The truth is, when you have a 'tude, you're griping and complaining nonverbally—usually because you're thinking about you and what you want to do—and that's what ends up getting you in trouble with your parents or your teachers or even your friends. When they see you roll your eyes or sneer, it's like you are saying something unkind with your body. And because nonverbal communication is the first thing people "read" on you, it is the thing that is often the loudest.

Philippians 2:5 says: "Your attitude should be the same as that of Christ Jesus" (NIV). Think about that for a minute—would Jesus roll his eyes at his mom? Do you think he would say unkind, ungrateful things nonverbally? No, we know that he didn't, and we need to strive to be more like him. Sometimes that is really hard, but you know what? God can help you with your attitude! He wants to help you. Start praying for help about your attitude and what your body says to others. Next time you feel that nasty, bad attitude creeping in, just whisper a prayer. Say, "God, let me have the same attitude as Jesus." Very soon you'll be saying "so long" to that bad 'tude'!✱

JUST BETWEEN US

1. Which people in your life tell you most often that you have a bad attitude? Why do you suppose they say that to you?

2. What situations do you think cause you to get in the most trouble with your attitude?

3. What is the root of your attitude issues? Selfishness? Wanting to be the boss? Laziness?

4. What is the first thing you should do when you realize you have had a bad attitude with someone?

PSSSt...
SoMEONE Is WatchiNG YoU

by Whitney Prosperi

Is there an older girl at your school or church that you really look up to? Maybe you want to talk, dress, and act like her because she seems so confident and cool. But here's a question: Have you ever thought that maybe someone younger is looking up to you? If you have a younger sister, brother, or cousin, they are watching you—just like you watch the older girls you know. Even if you don't have any younger relatives, someone you know is watching you. There may be a neighbor or girl who attends your church who thinks you are the absolute coolest person she knows. She wants to act just like you do. She listens as you talk to your friends and notices the things you wear. Think about that for a minute. If a younger girl decides to copy you, what kind of person will she become?

If you're an older sister, did you know that your brothers and sisters will treat your parents just like you do? If you talk back to them, they will talk back to them. If you disobey, they will disobey. You're a role model even if you don't want to be one. They will act just like you do. Even though your brothers and sisters may not tell you this, they secretly admire you. Really! *You.* Wow, if you think about it—that's a huge responsibility! Make sure that as they are following you, you are following Jesus.

First Timothy 4:12 tells us: "No one should despise your youth; instead, you should be an example to the believers in speech, in conduct, in love, in faith, in purity." Have you ever thought about the fact that the way you talk, dress, and even what you watch on TV will be repeated? How does that make you feel? Are there some changes you should make? Maybe you need to cut out the back talk to your parents. Or change the things you do online. Only you know what you should do to be a good role model.

Imagine that someone watched you all day, but you didn't know it. They secretly recorded all that you said and did. What kind of words did you say? Were you mean? Did you pass along a juicy piece of gossip? If a parent, teacher, or youth leader were to "grade" your behavior and attitude, what grade would you receive? Were you loving to your brothers and sisters? It's so easy to act mean or just ignore them. Maybe you need to apologize to someone in your family for something you said or did. If so, make sure you do that before you climb into bed.

A friend of mine became a Christian when she was about ten years old. Every day she left Bible verses in her little sister's room and told her about Jesus. She taught her songs and Bible stories so her little sister would know Jesus loved her. And one day she got to pray with her sister when she became a Christian. Instead of taking her little sister for granted, she chose to love her. Will you do the same? Remember that someone is watching you. Whether it's a sister, brother, cousin, or an admiring fan in your neighborhood or church, chances are, they want to be just like you. ✳

JUST BETWEEN US

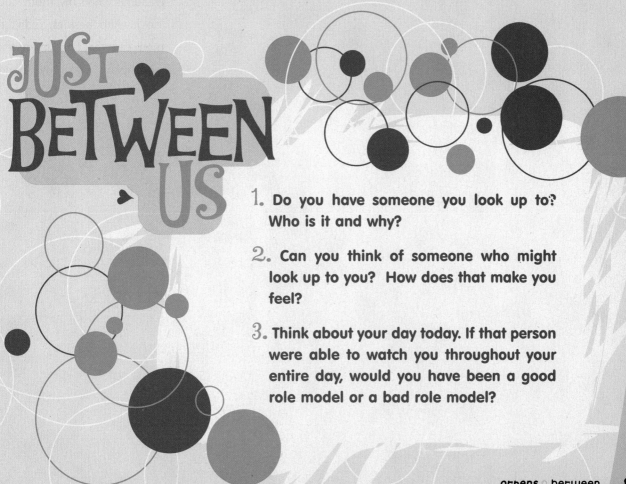

1. Do you have someone you look up to? Who is it and why?

2. Can you think of someone who might look up to you? How does that make you feel?

3. Think about your day today. If that person were able to watch you throughout your entire day, would you have been a good role model or a bad role model?

All Wigged Out

by SUSIE DAVIS

With a roll of my eyes,

I grabbed my car keys off the kitchen counter and walked toward the garage. My mother had given me the job of driving my grandmother to the local beauty center to buy her a new wig. My grandma had just moved in with our family because she was going through chemotherapy treatments for cancer. The chemo had caused her hair to fall out, and she wore wigs to cover her bald head.

Now I certainly didn't know why I should have to run this errand with my grandma when my mom could do it. And besides, didn't my mom care that I had made after school plans with my friends?

Didn't mom know that a sixteen-year-old, busy with high school activities, just didn't have time to drive her grandmother all the way across town to look at wigs?

Didn't she know that I was loaded up with homework? Didn't she know that a sixteen-year-old, busy with high school activities, just didn't have time to drive her grandmother all the way across town to look at wigs?

As we got in the car, I quickly turned up my music, hoping at least to enjoy the trip, and just as quickly my grandma started asking me about school.

"How is high school going for you, sweetie?"

"Fine," I replied.

"Do you like your classes?"

"Yes," I mumbled.

"Are you still dating that nice boy?"

"Uh-huh," I stammered.

as we started the trip home, I decided that speeding things up a little in the car would get us there sooner.

With the conversation going nowhere fast, she quietly hummed and looked out the window.

By the time we arrived at the beauty center, I was really hoping for some quick decision making on her part. From what I could tell by looking at my watch, if she decided on a wig quickly, I could meet up with my friends without being late. But my grandmother took her time, looking at this wig and that, asking what I thought about the style and color. I was growing more and more impatient.

Finally, a sales woman came over to help her make a decision. After trying on several, she carefully fitted my grandmother in the wig of her choice, and she paid for it. My grandmother was happy, and I was relieved.

As we started the trip home, I decided that speeding things up a little in the car would get us there sooner. I noticed my grandmother tightening her grip on the seat as I sped along. Finally, when she could no longer stand it, she asked me to slow down, and just as I was about to explain to her that I wasn't driving that fast, I took a corner too sharply and ran into a tree.

I got out of the car, checked the bumper, and wa relieved that there was no damage to the tree or the car. Then I got back in, apologized to my grandma, and drove carefully home.

That whole scene shook me up. Nearly wrecking your car at sixteen should, I suppose. But the thing that bothered me most was the fact that I was so impatient. So selfish. So uncaring. And so wigged out about a small change in my schedule. (You know, *wigged ou* as in "kind of crazy and thoughtless.") My schedule

nd my fun mattered more than everything else in my life—including my grandmother.

The Bible has some things to say about honoring people that are older or elderly. Leviticus 19:32 says: Show respect to the person with white hair. Honor n older person and you will honor your God. am the Lord" (NLV). Honestly, I wasn't hon- ring my grandmother with the way was acting. To honor someone is to respect hem, and then you show that you res- ect them through your actions. When we give someone respect, that means we are interested in pleas- ing them and placing their needs before our own. In my situation, I was doing nei- ther with my grandmother. Not only was I dishonoring her, I was dishonoring God.

The sad news is some years later, my grandma did eventually die of cancer. I'll never forget the phone call I got while I was away at college. My dad called late one night to tell me that she had slipped into a coma, which is kind of like being so sick that you are asleep and you can't be awakened. The doctor said that she wouldn't live much longer. Well, I was so upset about the call from my dad that I borrowed a friend's car and sped home, crying all the while.

When I arrived at the hospital, I quietly walked in to see my grandma. There she was, unable to say anything. I tenderly touched her hand and called her name.

I stood looking at her, as she was breathing very slowly, and remembered my time with her—the times we had laughed while playing a card game called "Pig,"

then I silently prayed.
I prayed that God would
forgive my ugly moments
with my grandma.

and the times we had enjoyed watching her favorite shows together. I also remembered the times I had arguments with her, the times I had been impatient and selfish.

Then I silently prayed. I prayed that God would forgive my ugly moments with my grandma. I prayed that he would forgive my impatience and my lack of concern. I prayed that she would know that I loved her. And then, through tears, I spoke to her.

"Grandma, I love you. I am so sad that you are in so much pain. Thank you for being such a great grandma. I also want you to know how sorry I am for not honoring you in all the ways I should. Please forgive me. Please let me know that you forgive me and you love me."

In the very next moment, her eyes fluttered and I felt her fingers lightly lift and touch my hand.

I leaned forward and hugged her tired body as gently as I could. She had spoken in the only way she could, letting me know that she forgave me and that she loved me.

Sometimes it is hard to always remember to honor the important people in your life. As a teenager, I didn't always do it right, but maybe you can learn from my mistakes.

Don't get wigged out, thinking only of yourself like I did the day my grandma needed a little help. Instead, think of ways to honor those people in your life by putting their needs in front of your own. Whether it is doing little errands for them or listening to their storie[s] fit some time into your day to care for them in a wa[y] that will show that you love them—and in that wa[y] you will honor God.

JUST BETWEEN US

1. Who are the "older people" or elders in your life? List three to five people who fit the description in Leviticus of having "white hair."

2. Think of one or two things you could do for those people to honor them. Write it down and make a plan to do it!

3. I was sad that I was so impatient with my grandmother, and I almost didn't get a chance to make things right with her. Is there someone in your life that is older who needs to hear an apology from you?

never★EVeR

Never Ever say ugly things about people and think that it will turn out well.

Never Ever ignore your friends just to get a boy to notice you.

Never Ever lie to your parents.

Never Ever yell at your siblings and tell them you hate them.

Never Ever forget to treat others as you would like to be treated.

Never Ever forget to thank people who take care of you.

Never Ever make your friends look stupid so you can look smart.

Never Ever watch a movie that your parents told you not to watch.

Never Ever think you're a baby if you need your parents to help you out in a tough situation.

Never Ever forget that gossip breaks up friendships. ✳

HA HA HA HA

Boy, Oh Boy!

by Susie Davis

Square dancing. I'm not quite sure why every school in America still teaches square dancing as a part of music, but I had to laugh when my sixth-grade daughter Sara popped into the car after school and started telling me all about the do-si-do situations she and her friends had with the boys! There was the "grand right and left" with all the different types of boy hands: dry, wet, clammy, rough, strong grasp, weak grasp, and the like. Then the oh-so-long promenade, when you are holding hands with your partner all the way around the corner. Gosh, it makes for lots of giggling fun for both the girls and the boys.

What is it about a boy that adds such interest to dancing? And who but boys could make square dancing fun? Boys—wonderful boys. In this article, you might just learn some new information about things you would never dream to ask about concerning those boys in your life. We'll cover some basic differences between boys and girls and maybe get closer to uncovering that oh-so-interesting reason why boys are the ideal dance partners for girls. But mainly, this article is designed to help you understand boys and then be able to get along better with them.

HA HA HA HA HA

Let's get started. You need to know that boys (even boys in third grade) have the basic set-up to become men—you know, men like your dad or your teenage cousin. They will grow hair just about all over their body, and their voice will deepen. And the reason this happens is because God made boys with a special something in their body called hormones. Hormones are invisible cell substances inside the body of every person that signal certain things to start happening. You have hormones. I have hormones. And boys have hormones. God created it that way. Now I'm not going to get into all the specifics of what each hormone does (there are several different types of hormones in humans!), but I can tell you that the reason boys turn into men is because of a hormone called testosterone. Testosterone creates maleness. And as girls, you are likely to think that maleness in your school-age friends (or cute boys on TV) is, well, nice. That is normal. But the problem comes in when you're not quite sure how to get along with them because of it. So here are the tips on how to get along with those testosterone types.

1st

One idea you need to keep in mind is that there is something I call body speed. Body speed is how fast or slow your body grows or matures. Usually at your age, boys and girls grow at different body speeds. Girls are usually growing faster than boys in fifth and sixth grade, which explains why girls are mostly taller than the boys their age. I don't know why it happens like that, but it just does. And not only are girls growing taller faster than boys, but they are also growing more mature on the inside. This explains why girls say to boys, **"You're so immature!"** You've probably heard that in the halls at school or in the lunchroom. And while that is likely true—that boys are somewhat less mature than you—it doesn't give you the right to rub their faces in it. In other words, you still need to be kind to the boys even if they seem to be bothersome because they are less grown up on the inside. In 2 Peter 1:7 it tells us to act in brotherly kindness, which in this situation, means that you should be kind to "your brothers," or in other words, the boys in your life. That would include no teasing, no laughing at, and no ugly words about their body speed. You know, like maybe laughing at them when their voice starts changing—and squeaking once in a while. The truth is that you don't control how fast or slow you are growing, and neither do they. So really, there is no reason to act superior about it. You are all growing at the exact speed that God designed, so be sure to be nice about it.

2nd

Remember that it is important to boys to be thought of as boys—or young "men in the making." The last thing they need or want is some girl making them feel stupid. Or like a sissy. That's just plain rude. Please give them a break by acting like a lady and not some mean girl (and I think you know what I mean here). Luke 2:52 says: **"And Jesus matured, growing up in both body and spirit, blessed by both God and people"** *(The Message).* When I read that verse, it occurred to me, Jesus had to grow up just the same as the boys around you. He grew in body and spirit. And just thinking of Jesus as a nine- or ten-year-old boy made me wonder if the girls that were in his life were nice to him. I sure hope so! But it also made me think about this: If Jesus was sitting in your classroom as a ten-year-old boy, would you feel as though you should treat him with brotherly kindness? Would you make sure to treat him as a little "man in the making"? I hope so. The Bible tells us that when we are kind to people, it is as if we are being kind to God himself. And when we are being ugly to someone, it is as if we are being ugly to God himself. ✱

Every last one of us is made in the image of God himself—both boys and girls. And we are all marvelously made in his image—just the way God intended.

Remembering that is a key to handling the boys in your life in the way God wants.

HA   HA   HA   HA

JUST BETWEEN US

1. When you think of the boys and girls in your class, do you see the "body speed" differences?

2. Do those differences cause problems sometimes? What types of problems?

3. How does treating boys with brotherly kindness help with some of the problems?

4. How would Jesus be treated if he was a boy your age at your school? Is that good or bad?

HA HA HA

HELP! My BEST FRIEND

by Vicki Courtney

BoyS, BoyS, BoyS.

ONE MINUTE THEY'RE FUN TO BE AROUND, AND THE NEXT MINUTE THEY'RE BURP-ING, BEING MEAN, AND ACTING SOOOOO IMMATURE. **It is perfectly normal to notice boys around your age. It is also perfectly normal not to notice boys around your age. Maybe you're one of the ones who doesn't care much about liking boys right now. Even if boys still make you think "Ick—cooties," chances are you have a friend or two (or three or four) who are completely and totally boy crazy.** You know, the girl whose life seems to center around what so-and-so said, or how he looked, or the way he smiled. She just can't stop talking about the boys

in your class. "He is WAY cute." "Who do you think so-and-so likes?" "Do you thinking he's looking at me?"

When I say "boy crazy," I'm not talking about the girl who has noticed boys and makes a comment every now and then. I'm talking about the girl who talks and thinks about boys now and then, and tomorrow, and the next day, and so on and so on. Do you know some-one like that? I bet you do. It can get on your nerves after awhile especially if you haven't really thought

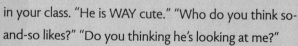

IS BOY CRAZY!

a lot about boys yet (except for the fact that they can be really annoying).

When I was your age, I was majorly boy crazy. I don't know if some girls are born more boy crazy than others, but if so, then I must have been one of them. I remember always picking out the "cute boys" in my class the first week of school each year. I even remember putting a note on a guy's desk in the fourth grade! In the note, I told him that I liked him and asked him who he liked. Yeah, I know—pretty bold, huh? He told one of my friends that he liked me, but we hardly talked for the rest of the year. It didn't matter. It was fun just knowing he liked me. My boy crazy days didn't end in fourth grade. I had my eye on another boy in fifth grade and another in sixth grade, and well, you get the picture.

You might wonder what the big deal is with being boy crazy at your age. For some girls it's a sign that they might not feel important unless they have a guy liking them and giving them attention. As they get older, they can focus on guys so much that they ignore other important things in their lives like their friends, schoolwork, and their relationship with God. There is a Bible verse that every girl should memorize whether she's boy crazy or not. **Proverbs 4:23 says: "Above all else, guard your heart, for it affects everything you do"** (NLT). As you get older, it's important that you learn to "guard your heart" from things that might take God's place in your heart. Even when you grow up and get married, you should love God more than anything or anyone else in the world. **Girls who are boy crazy at an early age sometimes grow up and let a guy's love become more important than God's love.**

> ABOVE ALL ELSE,
> GUARD YOUR HEART, FOR IT
> AFFECTS EVERYTHING YOU DO.
> PROVERBS 4:23 NLT

If one of your friends is going through a boy-crazy stage, there is very little you can do to make her change. **Don't give up on her. Pray for her and remember,** **you might not be able to get her to change, but God can.** The truth is, there's only one guy worth that much time and attention, and it's Jesus Christ. Ask God to help your friend understand how much Christ loves her. When the time is right, tell her (nicely) that you are worried that she is spending too much time thinking about boys. She might listen or she might not. And if you happen to be the boy-crazy one in this story, remember, there is no hurry. Take it from someone who was way too boy crazy, way too young. You have plenty of years ahead of you to think about boys. Enjoy being young. Enjoy your friends. **Most of all, enjoy thinking about how much you are loved by God!** ✳

JUST BETWEEN US

1. **Do you know girls who are boy crazy? Are you boy crazy?**

2. **What is the danger in being boy crazy?**

3. **How can girls your age "guard their hearts" from things that might take God's place?**

4. **How can you help your friends who are boy crazy?**

What's up with ... Barbie and ... Ken?

by Vicki Courtney

February 12, 2004, marked a very sad day for Barbie lovers, young and old. Just two days before Valentine's Day, an announcement was made in many newspapers that after forty-three happy years as America's most famous plastic couple, Barbie and Ken were splitting up. I laughed when I read it, but I'm sure that there were some girls who took it seriously, especially considering three Barbie dolls are sold every second around the world.

What is this world coming to when Barbie and Ken split? Barbie and Ken were supposed to be 2-gether 4-ever, period, end of sentence. Of course the whole Barbie and Ken breakup was a big joke, but it seemed to get funnier and funnier as the days went on. One newspaper said that they were breaking up because

Barbie's career had gotten in the way. Let's face it: the woman has had more than ninety careers, including a doctor, an astronaut, a paleontologist, an Olympic athlete, a fashion model, and a rock star. She even made a run for President! Or maybe the breakup

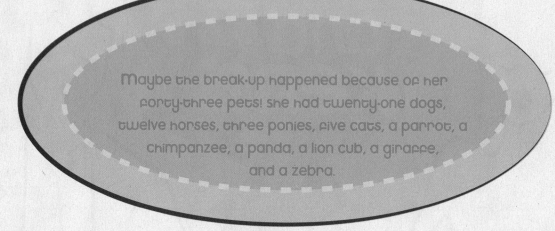

Maybe the break-up happened because of her forty-three pets! she had twenty-one dogs, twelve horses, three ponies, five cats, a parrot, a chimpanzee, a panda, a lion cub, a giraffe, and a zebra.

happened because of her forty-three pets! She had twenty-one dogs, twelve horses, three ponies, six cats, a parrot, a chimpanzee, a panda, a lion cub, a giraffe, and a zebra. Another newspaper joked and said that Barbie had a new boyfriend—some surfer dude from Australia named Blaine.

What young girl hasn't at some point marched her Barbie down a pretend aisle dressed in her lacy bridal gown and veil to say "I do" to her beloved Ken?

When I was a little girl, my friends and I would spend long hours preparing our Barbies for the dance that was to happen that evening. Every weekend was homecoming weekend in Barbie land. Barbie and her numerous Barbie look-alike friends would gather together at my best friend's Barbie mansion (I only had the pop-up camper) and spend the entire day getting ready for their dates. The big group of Kens would arrive on time in a parade of sports cars and jeeps, walk to the door, ring the doorbell, and gasp when our Barbies came down the staircase. They would walk our dolls to their cars and even open their car doors! After an evening of dancing in the arms of our Kens, our Barbies were escorted home, walked to the door, and some, but not all, received a light kiss on the cheek. Once inside, the slumber party began, and our Barbies stayed up giggling the night away over miniature fake popcorn and two-liter Cokes. It wasn't unusual for a wedding or two to follow the next day. We would all circle around and hum a chorus of dum, dum, da, dum when the lucky Barbie would make her way own the aisle. Of course we all giggled when they kissed after saying "I do." Even though it was pretend, we were all hoping that someday we would get a turn to walk down that aisle—not just in Barbie land but in real life.

Maybe we'll never know the real reason Barbie and Ken broke up. Wait a minute—can dolls break up?! Anyway, don't take it seriously, and most importantly, don't stop dreaming about the day you get to walk down the aisle in a beautiful wedding gown and say "I do." I know it's a long way off, but there's no harm in dreaming about it, right? And while you're at it, say a prayer for your future husband every now and then. God knows exactly who he is and can watch over him in the meantime. I wonder if his name will be Ken? ✳

JUST BETWEEN US

1. Do you ever dream about the day you will get married? Have you ever pretended as I did? If so, tell me about it!

2. Barbie and Ken's breakup was a big joke, but in real life couples do break up sometimes. By now you probably know what the word *divorce* means. Maybe your parents are divorced. If so, don't let that stop you from dreaming.

3. Most girls will grow up and get married. There is nothing wrong with praying for your future husband—even though you probably have not met him yet! Stop and say a prayer for him right now.

CHAPTER 3: GOD

Talk to the

by Susie Davis

Dr. Doolittle is such a funny story. When I was little, I remember wishing that I could talk to the animals. Wouldn't it be weird to hear your dog talk back to you? Or hear your cat complain? I think my dogs would tell me to bring them inside more often, or maybe they would ask me to come outside and play with them. (Really, they would just ask for more treats.) It would be interesting to know what in the world they are thinking about when they look up at me and wag those tails. Can you even imagine it?

Do you know the really amazing thing? In the Bible in the book of Job, God told Job he could learn a thing or two from the animals. Job 12:7–10 says, **"Ask the animals, and they will teach you. Ask the birds of the sky, and they will tell you. Speak to the earth, and it will instruct you. Let the fish of the sea speak to you. They all know that the Lord has done this. For the life of every living thing is in his hand, and the breath of all humanity"** (NLT).

Isn't that crazy? To think that God not only made all these hundreds and hundreds of animals, but he also designed them to teach us things. I love that about God because I am a real animal lover. In my family right now, we have two dogs (labs), a rabbit (dwarf), a bird (parakeet), and a horse (thoroughbred). We have also had guinea pigs and hamsters. We have enjoyed every single animal that finds a place in our home. Each one is different, with its own unique personality (the rabbit can be down right scary at mealtime!) and look (our black lab is especially handsome).

ANIMALS

But ask the animals what they think—let them teach you.

Job 12:7 (*The Message*)

Now animals don't speak with words, but they still have something to say. By just observing them, we can learn from them. They can teach us useful things by watching and studying them.

For example, our mare Molly Brown is a bay thoroughbred. She is about sixteen years old, and I ride her several times a week. Every time I go to saddle her up, she stands willingly. When I get on her and take her out to the riding arena, she will walk, trot, canter, or jump obstacles at my command. I direct her with the reins and my legs just sitting pretty in the saddle while she does all the hard work. She does not complain or refuse; rather, she keeps on working. Whether it's hot or cold, dry or rainy, Molly is ready to work hard at my command. Pretty amazing. I reward her by providing a nice place for her to live with lots of grain, hay, and green grass to munch on. But the truth is she doesn't work for a reward. She's just a hard worker. And we can learn from her. **Colossians 3:23 says, "Work hard and cheerfully at whatever you do, as though you were working for the Lord rather than for people"** (NLT). It's a great verse, and I bet Molly would like it if she could understand it because she is such a hard

> Now animals don't speak with words, but they still have something to say.

god o between   **105**

worker. She is a lesson to me that I should work hard and with a good attitude, remembering that all my work is for God.

Another animal in my family that teaches me about God is Mango, our parakeet. She is a little green and yellow bird that sings and chirps and sometimes even squawks! She's a real noisemaker. But her specialty is singing. We cover her cage at night with a towel to let her know it's time to go to sleep. And every morning, even before we uncover her, she starts chirping and singing. That bird will sing and sing until we uncover her! It's like she just can't wait to get the morning started. She can't wait to get her songs out to anyone who will listen. **And whenever I hear her, I remember a verse in Psalm 150:6 that says, "Let everything that has breath praise the LORD" (NIV). The truth is, you and I have "breath" just as Mango has breath.** It's the thing that keeps us alive! And the verse says that as long as we're all breathing, we should praise the Lord. Just as Mango is hard to keep quiet, we should learn from her and keep singing God's praises!

Finally, I learn from my yellow lab, Mary Spoon (weird name—long story). Awhile back I acciden-tally ran over her in my car. (I know, I know—it was really bad!) She was sleeping under my car in the garage, and I started backing out without realizing she was under it. The good news is, she wasn't hurt. The better news is, she didn't hold a grudge. Right after we

got her out from under the car, she ran straight up to me and licked my hand. She stood by my side as if nothing had happened. Now I know that dogs aren't as smart as humans, and I really don't think they are smart enough to understand forgiveness; but I have to tell you that every time I see that dog, I am reminded of how she acted after I ran over her. I am also reminded of Ephesians 4:32, which says, **"Forgive one another as quickly and thoroughly as God in Christ forgave you" (The Message).** Mary Spoon reminds me to forgive and to do it quickly the way God forgives me. That dog is some kind of Bible teacher!

What about you? Can you learn from the animals? What might the animals in your life say to you? Try observing the animals around you and think about

how they act. Then read the Bible and see if God just might use an animal to teach you a thing or two. ✳

JUST BETWEEN US

1. Where do you "work"? How can you work hard and cheerfully at the jobs you have been assigned (like school, chores, etc.)?

2. Do this little test. Pinch your nose closed with one hand. Now open your mouth and put your other hand in front of it. Now what do you feel? (Your breath!) Reread this verse: "Let everything that has breath praise the Lord." What does that mean you should be doing?

3. Mary Spoon taught me to remember and try to be quick to forgive. Are you quick to forgive? Pray and ask God to help you remember Ephesians 4:32. You might even want to memorize it.

4. Have you ever considered that animals can teach about God things? List any animals you have and then write down what you think they can teach you about God.

survey: Dear God...

we asked girls your age this question: if you could ask God one question and get an answer right away, what would it be?

God, why do my brothers go crazy when I have friends over?
Nicole, age 11

God, what should I do while I wait for you to bring me a best friend at school?
Lydia, age 9

God, what's it like to be a kitty?
Hannah, age 9

God, why did you make allergies?
Zoe, age 10

God, do people have birthdays in heaven?
Faith, age 11

God, why didn't you let Jesus stay on earth to get married and have children?
Natalie, age 8

God, what made you want to give your only Son for so many people?
Ivy, age 11

God, what is your favorite color?
Alyssa, age 10

God, how did you feel when you were on the cross?

Alexandria, age 10

God, why do people get divorced?

Faith, age 9

God, where will I be in ten years? What will my life be like?

Claire, age 10

God, are tomatoes a fruit or a vegetable?

Abbey, age 10

God, how old are you? Did you just appear? Who is your mom?

Eleni, age 9

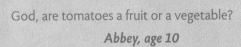

God, how did you dream up every human and their personalities?

Lisa, age 11

God, how did you make the world?

Taylor, age 8

God, will I ever get a baby brother or sister?

Megan, age 9

God, how did you make rainbows?

Samantha, age 9

God, what does heaven look like?

Jordanne, age 10

God, why do people smoke?

Melissa, age 11

God, why did you make lightning?

Casey, age 8

God, what does it feel like to rule the world?

Haley, age 9

God, will I make it into Harvard University in Boston, MA?

Natalia, age 10

God, who will I marry when I grow up?

Gabrielle, age 10

TREASURE SEEKER

by SUSIE DAVIS

WHEN I WAS LITTLE, I WOULD BEG my mom TO BUY CERTAIN CEREALS AT THE GROCERY STORE. It was usually the delicious sugary stuff like Captain Crunch or Sugar Pops. My mom barely ever bought that type of cereal because she knew that what I was really after was the toy inside the box. Sometimes when she did buy the cereal I was begging for, the minute I got home I would sink my hand deep into the open box, my fingers

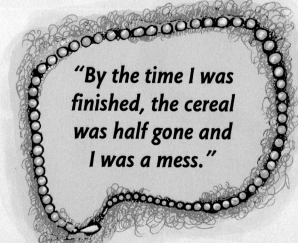

"By the time I was finished, the cereal was half gone and I was a mess."

searching for the prize. As I pushed my little fingers down further and further through the cereal, anxious to find the toy, cereal would always spill out over the top. With my arm stuffed in the box, I would smile with satisfaction when I could finally feel the edges of the bag that held the prize I was after. Slowly I would pull the toy up through the cereal, which continued to spill out all around me. By the time I was finished, the cereal was half gone, and I was a mess. There were even times when I would search and search, unable to find the prize, and would finally dump all the cereal in a big bowl just so I could find the toy. Then I would carefully try to pour the cereal back in the bag, happy to have found the prize. Finally my mom (frustrated by the way I was wasting cereal because I was spilling it out all the time) would make me wait until the cereal was used up the regular way, with people eating it for breakfast. That was always the worst. And you can be sure that I was eating tons of that stuff just to get the level of the cereal down so I could spot the prize and pull it out. I would do *anything* to get that *treasure*.

There is nothing more amazing and mysterious than treasure. Though it seems like something we would only find in movies or books like *Treasure Island*, did you know that the Bible talks about treasure? As a matter of fact, the writer of the Psalms states that the Word of God is just like pure gold!

Psalm 119:140 says, "Your word to me, your servant, is like pure gold; I treasure what you say" (CEV). **And in Psalm 119:162 the writer exclaims, "I rejoice over Your promise like one who finds vast treasure."** Vast treasure—that means treasure that is great in size or amount. Pretty amazing, isn't it? Real treasure—the Bible—sitting right there on your bookshelf.

And yet, to be honest, if you're like me, sometimes you don't feel like the Bible is that important. I mean, like riches? If I really thought about the Bible like that, I would be running to read it or scrambling to get at it—kind of like I did with the prize in the cereal box. But maybe we're missing something by not thinking of the Bible in that way.

Are you curious how to find some treasure in the Word of God? Would you like to think of the Bible as gold? If you want to be a treasure seeker, then you might try doing some of the following. First, you need

to believe that God's Word is a treasure that can change your life. Anytime we read the Bible, we can count on it making important changes in the way we think, which will affect the way we act. When we think right and act right, that's called wisdom, and wisdom is completely valuable. It keeps you out of trouble. It increases your understanding of God. It makes your life better. Wisdom is a treasure in life that can be even better than having the kind of gold you can hold in your hands.

Second, make sure you have a Bible that you can easily understand. If you don't, see if you can go to the bookstore for one. And if you still have trouble with certain books of the Bible (sometimes even grown-ups have trouble understanding the Bible!) then

ask your mom or dad or someone at church to help you understand what you are reading. Maybe even look into getting a devotional just for kids. (Look at the section below for some ideas on devotionals.) What is the best time in your day for you to read the Bible? Write it down and consider it your appointment with God.

Third, you just need to jump in and get busy reading the Bible. The main part of being a treasure seeker of God's Word is to realize that to get the most reward you will need to decide to read the Bible every day. Now that might seem impossible, but you can do it! Just like you know you will brush your teeth for the rest of your life or wash your hair for the rest of your life, you can commit

"Your word to me, your servant, is like pure gold; I treasure what you say."
Psalm 119:140 (CEV)

"I rejoice over Your promise like one who finds vast treasure."
Psalm 119:162

reading the Bible for the rest of your life. Just take it one day at a time. And ask God to help you. Pray the following prayer if you'd like to read your Bible for the rest of your life:

Dear God,

I know that your Word is a treasure, and I want that treasure in my life. I want to know you better, and I realize your story is in the pages of the Bible.

Please God, help me to read the Bible every day and give me lots of wisdom. Help me love the Bible. Thank you for the Bible. Thank you for caring about me and my life. Thank you for loving me. Amen.

Finally, remember to jump in and be a treasure seeker! And then be on the lookout in your life for all kinds of treasure to pop up.

1. Why is it hard to imagine the Bible as real treasure?

2. Can you think of a time when you read God's Word and it helped you stay out of trouble? If yes, how valuable was God's Word to you in that situation?

3. Why does getting treasure out of the Bible require that we read the Bible often?

4. How often do you read the Bible?

5. Set up a time every day to read a section of the Bible or a devotional. What time of day is the best time for you to read?

Devotionals are books that teach people about God. They usually have some Bible verses and some thoughts about living a Christian life. Reading a devotional book is a great way to start getting to know the Bible better. Try some of these devotionals:

Girlz Rock Devotions for You
The One Year Book of Devotions for Girls
Jesus Wants All of Me: Daily Devotional for Kids!

QUIZ

PRAYER POP QUIZ

by Vicki Courtney

1. God won't hear your prayers unless you fold your hands and close your eyes.

    True   False

2. The main reason we pray is to ask God for stuff.

    True   False

3. The Lord's Prayer (Our Father, who art in heaven . . .) is a prayer that Jesus taught his disciples to pray.

    True   False

4. It is a good idea to pray in front of other people so you can prove that you are religious.

    True   False

5. The Bible says to pray for our enemies.

    True   False

6. The Bible tells us that if we don't know what to pray for, the Holy Spirit will talk to God for us.

    True   False

7. The Bible tells us that if we are suffering, we should pray.

  True   False

8. The Bible says to pray continually (take thought of God throughout our day).

  True   False

9. God doesn't listen to all our prayers.

  True   False

10. God takes delight in our prayers.

  True   False

ANSWERS

1. FALSE You can pray anytime and anywhere. Jude 1:20 says, "But you, dear friends, must continue to build your lives on the foundation of your holy faith. And continue to pray as you are directed by the Holy Spirit." If God had wanted us to fold our hands and close our eyes every time we pray, he would have mentioned it in the Bible.

2. FALSE Prayer is about communicating with God and growing closer to him. We should always pray with an attitude that says, "Your kingdom come, your will be done on earth as it is in heaven."

3. TRUE In the King James Version of the Bible, Matthew 6:9–13 says, "After this manner therefore pray ye: Our Father which art in heaven, Hallowed be thy name. Thy kingdom come. Thy will be done in earth, as it is in heaven. Give us this day our daily bread. And forgive us our debts, as we forgive our debtors. And lead us not into temptation, but deliver us from evil: For thine is the kingdom, and the power, and the glory, for ever. Amen."

4. FALSE Matthew 6:5–6 says, "And now about prayer. When you pray, don't be like the hypocrites who love to pray publicly on street corners and in the synagogues where everyone can see them. I assure you, that is all the reward they will ever get. But when you pray, go away by yourself, shut the door behind you, and pray to your Father secretly. Then your Father, who knows all secrets, will reward you.

5. TRUE Matthew 5:44 says, "But I say, love your enemies! Pray for those who persecute you!"

6. TRUE Romans 8:26 says, "And the Holy Spirit helps us in our distress. For we don't even know what we should pray for, nor how we should pray. But the Holy Spirit prays for us with groanings that cannot be expressed in words."

7. TRUE James 5:13 says, "Are any among you suffering? They should keep on praying about it. And those who have reason to be thankful should continually sing praises to the Lord."

8. TRUE Ephesians 6:18 says, "Pray at all times and on every occasion in the power of the Holy Spirit. Stay alert and be persistent in your prayers for all Christians everywhere."

9. FALSE Psalm 66:19 says, "But God did listen! He paid attention to my prayer."

10. TRUE Proverbs 15:8 says, "The LORD hates the sacrifice of the wicked, but he delights in the prayers of the upright."

All Scripture references except #3 are from the New Living Translation.

GOD is not a vending machine

by
Vicki Courtney

Have you ever stayed in a hotel? You know how they have soda machines and ice makers on almost every floor? Have you noticed the machines that have all the snacks? For only sixty-five cents you could have just about any snack you can think of. That's all you have to do: put your money in and make your selection. D-5. Then those peanut butter crackers or M&Ms or Cheetos are yours! It's that easy.

Sometimes we can treat praying kind of like a vending machine. We give God our prayers, and we expect him to give us what we asked for. Unfortunately, praye doesn't really work that way. Let me tell you a littl about how I learned about prayer.

When I was little, I used to pray "wish-list prayers to God. They were kind of like quarters I would pu in the vending machine, hoping I would get wha I punched in. "God, I'll take an 'A' on my test tomo row." Each night I went over my list of wants with Goc It went something like this:

ACTS

Dear God,

Please, please, please help me remember my spelling words even though I didn't really study. And please let Mark like me and not Missy. And please make my brother vanish into thin air. Amen.

As I went on to middle school, my prayers were still all about what I wanted: making the cheerleading squad, winning track meets, getting invited to the cool kids' houses, and praying my parents wouldn't find out I got in trouble for passing notes in class.

By high school it was clear that he didn't always answer my prayers in the way I wanted. I had pretty much decided that he either (a) must not be listening or (b) must not care. Either way, I didn't think that praying worked, so my prayers basically stopped except for when I was in real big trouble. Then I might say a prayer to God to see if it got any results.

When I finally became a Christian in college, I figured out that I had a lot to learn about prayer. Someone taught me the ACTS model of prayer. ACTS stands for Adoration, Confession, Thanks, and Supplication. (The first letters spell the word *acts*.) People of any age can use this model. In fact, I still use this method today!

The ACTS Prayer Model:

Adoration

The "A" of ACTS stands for *adoration*. Adoration simply means to brag on God. We should start prayer by praising God for how awesome he is. When you pray, start by remembering what you love about God and "adoring" him for those things. Examples would be praising him for his perfection, his enormous power, his ability to forgive us, his control of all the earth and the skies, his desire to love us completely, his gift of Jesus, etc. The list goes on and on! You can praise God for anything. Praising God—adoration—helps us take the focus off ourselves and direct our attention to God.

ConFession

The "C" of ACTS stands for *confession*. Confession is basically telling God about when we've done something wrong and feeling sorry for it. When I get to the confession part of my prayer time, I try to think of specific ways that I have been wrong that day rather than simply saying, "Forgive me for my sins." An example would be: "Lord, I confess that I was wrong when I had a bad attitude when my mom asked me to unload the dishwasher." If

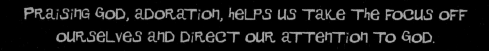

PRAISING GOD, ADORATION, HELPS US TAKE THE FOCUS OFF OURSELVES AND DIRECT OUR ATTENTION TO GOD.

my confession involves a sin against another person (Mom, in this case), many times God uses my prayer time to direct me to talk with that person and ask their forgiveness. Confessing our sin every day helps us to remember that sin is serious to God. As you confess your sins to God, remember that no sin is too big for him to forgive. Our part is to admit our sin. His part is forgiveness (see 1 John 1:9).

Thanks

The "T" in ACTS stands for *thanks*. I bet you can think of the one holiday when it is easy to remember to thank God for his blessings. That's right! Thanksgiving. I love Thanksgiving not only because of the annual turkey and pumpkin pie feast but also because, as a family,

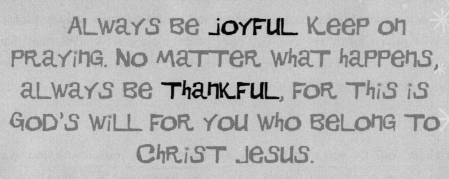

ALWAYS BE JOYFUL. KEEP ON PRAYING. NO MATTER WHAT HAPPENS, ALWAYS BE THANKFUL, FOR THIS IS GOD'S WILL FOR YOU WHO BELONG TO CHRIST JESUS.

1 Thessalonians 5:16–18 NLT

We offer thanks to God for what he has given us. We also thank him for the prayers he has answered (even if it wasn't the answer we wanted). Did you know that we're supposed to have Thanksgiving all year long? That's right; every day should be Thanksgiving, with or without the turkey and dressing!

It is easy to forget to thank God on a regular basis. One way to remember is to use a prayer journal. Start by taking a notebook, journal, or even a piece of paper and make a list of things you are thankful for, like your church, your friends, your parents, or for your brothers or sisters (yes, even if they do drive you crazy!). If you can't think of anything, you should always be thankful for God's Son, Jesus, who died on the cross for you. With all that we have been blessed with, we should have no problem thinking of things to thank God for.

In addition to thanking God for the blessings he gives us, we should also thank him for answering our prayers. Begin by taking that same prayer journal, or notebook, and divide the pages into two columns. In one column, list your prayer requests, and in the other column, mark how or when the prayer was answered, even if the answer was "no!" (The Bible tells us to be thankful in all circumstances [see 1 Thessalonians 5:18].)

SUPPLICATION

The "S" in ACTS stands for *supplication*. Supplication means asking God for something for ourselves or for others. When you ask God for things, try to think of others first, and lift up your own needs last. This is the part of prayer where you talk to God about your grandmother who is sick, or your dad who needs a new job, or maybe your best friend whose parents are getting a divorce. After you say your prayers for others, then you can pray for yourself. Be honest with God. Are you sad? Tell him. Are you scared? Tell him. Talk to him as you would your very best friend, and remember that you prayers are heard. Sometimes God doesn't answer ou prayer in the way we would like. Like the time I praye and prayed to make seventh-grade cheerleader, bu I didn't make it. Now I understand that God's ways ar higher than our ways.

So, what about you? Do you treat God like a vending machine when it comes to prayer? If so, you're missing out on what prayer is all about. Put your change away and try using the ACTS model. It is important that you talk with God on a daily basis. Yo don't have to wait till bedtime to say your prayers. Ge in the habit of talking to him throughout your day a things come up. He can't wait to talk to you. ✱

JUST BETWEEN US

1. Have you ever treated prayer like a vending machine?

2. What are some things you adore about god?

3. Name something that you need to confess to god.

4. What are three things you are thankful for?

5. What are some requests you would like to make to god?

Congratulations! You just completed the ACTS model of prayer! See how easy it is? Try to get in the habit of using it each day.

never ever :::

Never Ever forget that God loves you.

Never Ever believe that God will stop loving you.

Never Ever forget that God happily grants forgiveness to those who ask.

Never Ever think you can make God forget about you.

Never Ever accept the lie that you have to be perfect for God to love you.

Never Ever believe that the devil is stronger than God.

Never Ever feel as though you have to ask God to save you over and over again. Once is enough.

Never Ever forget God has assigned angels to watch over you.

Never Ever forget the Bible will help you with your everyday problems.

HAVING a GRATEFUL HEART

by SUSIE DAVIS

Do you ever wish you were really good at something? Sometimes I do. When I hear certain musicians, I listen in amazement at how they are able to sing so beautifully. (I sing along, sounding nothing like them at all!)

Often when I look at paintings, I imagine I can paint just like the artist and create designs that inspire people. Or when people are really smart, I often sit in awe listening to the things they say. It can be very motivating to be around people who are really good at something.

One of my big ideas this year is to be really good at the things God thinks are important. Have you ever stopped to think about what God thinks of as important? It is not always the same kinds of things we think of as important.

God likes things like love, patience, peace, and joy. I want to be good at those things because I know that they are important to God. But another one I really want to work on is gratitude because in Colossians 3:15 the Bible says we should be grateful.

Gratitude is being aware of the things you receive and giving thanks for them. And while it is easy to enjoy the things you receive, it is sometimes harder to stay thankful for them. Here's what I mean . . .

Think back to Christmas or your birthday. There were probably one or two things you really wanted. You asked for that special something and hoped that your parents or grandparents would take your continual hints to heart: "I'd really love an iPod! It would be so fun to have one, and then I would be so happy. There's nothing I would rather have than an iPod." Then that happy moment comes, and you open the sought-after gift. You delight in the new gift with a grateful, contented heart. And you give out lots of big hugs to let the giver know how much you appreciate it.

But now fast-forward two or three months. You've had that iPod for a while, and though you still manage to enjoy it every day or so, you've stopped thanking your parents or grandparents for it. That's pretty normal. **We all get used to having things around that we enjoy. But sometimes we get so used to the gifts that we forget to have a grateful heart about them. That's called "taking things for granted."**

But gratitude can change that. Being good at gratitude means you are able to remember all the nice things

you have been given, and you maintain a thankful attitude. It means you appreciate the people in your life too and thank them for all they do for you. And you know what? That makes everyone happy—especially God.

Why not think about becoming really good at one of the things God loves, like gratitude. Get a little notepad, and before you go to bed every night, write down ten things that make you feel grateful. After a week or so, look over your list, and you'll begin to remember all the blessings in your life in a new way.

It can make your life more fun, and you just might inspire some people along the way by being really good at some of the things that matter most to God.

JUST BETWEEN US

1. God gives us people who take care of us. Who are three people who take care of you? How might you show gratitude toward them for all they do for you?

2. God blesses us with all kinds of things that make us happy. Write down three things that you really love. Is taking care of things without complaining a way to show gratitude?

3. Having a grateful heart takes practice. Start thanking people when they do nice things for you, like making your breakfast or doing your hair. Or helping you at school with a difficult math problem or saving your seat at the lunch table. See how many people you can say "thank you" to today.

4. How does expressing thankfulness make you feel? How about others around you? How do you think it makes God feel?

JUST ASK!
YOUR QUESTIONS ABOUT GOD

by Vicki Courtney

 Q: How many people can fit into heaven? (Catherine, age 8)

Q: Why doesn't God answer some prayers? (Megan, age 9)

A: Since God created heaven, it will be plenty big enough to hold all those who believe in his Son, Jesus! In fact, the Bible tells us that there are many mansions, and God prepares a place for each of us!

A: God always answers prayer. He just doesn't always answer in the way we want him to. Be sure to read "God Is Not a Vending Machine" on page 116 to understand this better. Look at it this way: when we pray, God says "yes," "no," or "wait." We might not agree with the way he answers, but he always answers.

Q: Why does God like some people more than other people? (Mikayla, age 10)

A: God loves us all just the same. I know it's hard to believe since people usually have favorites. God created each and every one of us, and even though we sometimes disappoint him, he never stops loving us. You know how some teachers seem to like the smart kids in the class better? Well, God is not like that. I know it's hard to believe, but he doesn't even like the ones who are serving him better than the ones who are not. He loves you just as much as he loves your pastor. Pretty amazing, huh?

Q: When is the rapture coming? (Alexandra, age 10)

A: When Jesus lived on the earth (as a man), he told his disciples that he would someday return again and that his return would signal the end of the world. The word we use for the return of Jesus is *rapture*. Here is how the Bible describes the rapture in Matthew 24:30–31:

"And then at last, the sign of the coming of the Son of Man will appear in the heavens, and there will be deep mourning among all the nations of the earth. And they will see the Son of Man arrive on the clouds of heaven with power and great glory. And he will send forth his angels with the sound of a mighty trumpet blast, and they will gather together his chosen ones from the farthest ends of the earth and heaven" (NLT).

One day the disciples asked Jesus if there would be some kind of sign to know when his return and the end of the world would take place. In Matthew 24, Jesus told them that there will be signs like famines (starvation), earthquakes, and wars around the world. He also said that sin would be everywhere and the love of man would grow cold. False prophets (people who claim to know God's truth but are fakes) would be everywhere. Finally, he said that the gospel (the message that Jesus died on the cross for our sins) would be preached everywhere before the end of the world. He reminded the disciples that even when all those signs occurred, he might not return right away. In Matthew 24:36, he said this: "However, no one knows the day or the hour when these things will happen, not even the angels in heaven or the Son himself. Only the Father knows."

Christians should not worry about these things because they will survive the end of the world and spend eternity with God in heaven. The end of the world may or may not happen in your lifetime. It may be hundreds or even thousands of years away. The most important thing Jesus tells us about his return is to be prepared. If you are a Christian, you are prepared. It should also inspire us to tell other people about Jesus (the gospel: Jesus died on the cross for our sins).

Q: How did the people who wrote the Bible know what to write? (Anna, age 11)

A: That's a great question! The Bible has many authors, but God is the one who gave people the words to write. In 2 Timothy 3:16, Scripture says, "All Scripture is inspired by God and is useful to teach us what is true" (NLT). In order for the Bible to be true, it had to come from God!

There are two different ways he inspired the writers. The first way was to speak to them directly. In the Old Testament, or first part of your Bible, God often would speak out loud to certain people, like Moses or the prophets.

Also, in the first four books of the New Testament (the Gospels), people recorded Jesus' actual words. Those are examples of God directly speaking to people. In other cases, we know that God inspired them indirectly by putting things in their hearts. You know how you sometimes get a great idea out of nowhere? That's kind of how God worked with those people. He gave them the words to write and put it in their heart.

Q: How do I know for sure that I'm going to heaven? (Zoe, age 9)

A: You can be certain that you are going to heaven if you believe that Jesus died on the cross for your sins and you have accepted God's gift of forgiveness. If you are not sure about it, read "A Hummer of a Deal" on page 146 and "And the Winner Is . . . You!" on page 148.

Q: How is God three people at once (Father, Son, Holy Spirit)? (Kara, age 12)

A: Look at it like this. The real name for the water you drink is H_2O. You will learn more about this in science. H_2O can be in three forms: water, steam, and ice. It is the same way with God. He can be in the form of Father, Son, or Holy Spirit (some Christians say "Holy Ghost"). In the Bible we learn about God, the loving Father. We also learn about how God came to earth in the form of a perfect sinless man (Jesus, the Son), and we learn how God is also the Holy Spirit. The Holy Spirit is what we have to help us know right from wrong. When Jesus rose from the dead, he came back briefly and told his disciples that even though he was going back to heaven (to sit at God's side and prepare a place for us), he was leaving the Holy Spirit as a helper. Sometimes you might hear people say, "Does God's Spirit live in your heart?" That's what that means. If you have accepted God's gift of forgiveness in Christ, you have his Spirit living in your heart. He (the Holy Spirit) helps you know right from wrong and sets you apart as God's child.

Q: How can God be everywhere at one time? (Tiffany, age 11)

A: That is one of the mysteries of God. No matter how hard we try to understand it, we won't be able to. Nothing is impossible with God. He is omniscient (all-knowing) and omnipresent (everywhere at once), which should bring us great comfort. Whenever and wherever we need him, he is there.

Q: Did God make dinosaurs, and why are they not in the Bible? (Bridgette, age 11)

A: Yes! Genesis tells us that on day six, God created all land animals, and that includes dinosaurs. Some people think that dinosaurs are mentioned in the Bible. For instance, there are Hebrew words such as *Tanniyn, behemoth,* and *leviathan* found in the Old Testament that many people think refer to dinosaurs (Job 40:15–24; Job 41; Psalm 104:25–26 Isaiah 27:1).

Q: How do you know if you've lived a good enough life to go to heaven? (Libby, age 9)

A: The only way you can be certain you are going to heaven is to believe in Jesus Christ with all your heart and believe that God sent him to die on the cross for your sins (the wrong things you have done). The truth is, you can't live a good enough life to go to heaven. God wants us to do good things, but those good things will not get us into heaven. We need to be perfect (like God), and no matter how good we are, we will not be perfect. Only the forgiveness of Jesus will make us perfect in God's eyes. To understand it better, be sure to read "And the Winner Is . . . You!" on page 148.

Q: Will God heal my arthritis? I have faith in God. (Kaylee, age 10)

A: Kaylee, one of the girls in my office has arthritis, so I asked her to answer your question. Here is what Susan had to say:

You know what, Kaylee? I want to know that very thing myself! When I was just a little older than you, my doctor told me that I had arthritis too. It hurt so bad I wanted the pain to go away as quickly as possible. And I really wanted to know if I was going to have arthritis forever! My mom and I would pray for healing, but we also believed and had faith that God had a purpose for my arthritis. Over the years God has not decided to heal my body (yet), but he has given me SO much more! I have learned how to stay strong through really tough times. In James 1:2–4, the Bible says, *"Dear brothers and sisters, whenever trouble comes your way, let it be an opportunity for joy. For when your faith is tested, your endurance has a chance to grow. So let it grow, for when your endurance is fully developed, you will be strong in character and ready for anything"* (cai).

That's a long verse that means by making it through rough times in life (especially physical pain), God is perfecting your character. He's making you to be more like him, and it is only through your faith that he can work. Your life can be such an encouragement to others around you too. So keep the faith, Kaylee. Even if God does not heal your body (which I, too, pray he will), know that he loves you and is pleased by your faith in him no matter what. He is good.

DEAR BROTHERS AND SISTERS, WHENEVER TROUBLE COMES YOUR WAY, LET IT BE AN OPPORTUNITY FOR JOY. FOR WHEN YOUR FAITH IS TESTED, YOUR ENDURANCE HAS A CHANCE TO GROW. SO LET IT GROW, FOR WHEN YOUR ENDURANCE IS FULLY DEVELOPED, YOU WILL BE STRONG IN CHARACTER AND READY FOR ANYTHING. JAMES 1:2–4

Q: Do you eat in heaven? (Hannah, age 12)

A: In heaven we won't have our bodies. The Bible talks about our bodies being like a "tent" (2 Corinthians 5:4) and that we will shed them when we die and exchange them for a new "heavenly body." I'm not sure what that really means, but I doubt we will need to eat! I know it's hard to imagine what heaven will be like since earth is all we know. Sometimes I joke about my "mansion" in heaven and say that I hope I can have my very own Starbucks coffee shop in it! I love grande vanilla lattes from Starbucks, but truthfully, I won't need Starbucks to be happy. I will have Jesus and that's all I need. :)

do you have what it takes?

by Susie Davis

"**Do you have what it takes to become the next American Idol?**" The familiar words echoed through the family room as my daughters turned up the volume, readying to watch American Idol. It is one of the programs on TV that my whole family enjoy together. We listen and laugh and try to guess who will make it through to the next round. As the weeks pass, we watch with excitement, wondering (and a few of my family members voting!) who will become the next "American Idol."

It's an interesting and entertaining show. But have you ever really thought about what the word *idol* means? In this case the show revolves around everyone trying to become the idol. It is the desired thing to achieve. To become the idol means that everyone thinks you're fabulous! Instantly popular. Instantly on the cover of every newspaper. And instantly winning a recording contract. In the Bible, God talks a lot about idols, and it's not at all like the show.

In Leviticus 26:1 God says, "Do not make idols or set up carved images, sacred pillars, or shaped stones to be worshiped in your land. I, the LORD, am your God" (NLT). God is commanding the people *not to make idols*. In those days it wasn't unusual for someone to grab a stone, carve it, and set it up as something to be worshipped or adored. I know it sounds pretty silly, but that was the custom back then, and God didn't like it. The reason he didn't like it is because he wanted to be worshipped and adored. God stills wants to be worshipped as first place in our life all the time—just as he did with the people in the Old Testament. So he addressed the problem of idolatry all through the Old and New Testaments.

Deuteronomy 11:16 says, "But do not let your heart turn away from the Lord to worship other gods" (NLT). The gods in this case were anything other than the Lord God, like the carved stones. And though it is unbelievable to think of worshipping a stone carved by a man and making a god out of it, the truth is, we have a tendency to make idols out of things these days too.

what's my idol?

> *Do not make idols or set up carved images, sacred pillars, or shaped stones to be worshiped in your land. I, the LORD, am your God.*
>
> *Leviticus 26:1*
>
> *But do not let your heart turn away from the Lord to worship other gods.*
>
> *Deuteronomy 11:16*

often? Then ask yourself if that thing takes a higher place in your life than God.

It could be a sports activity. Or a hobby. Maybe even a friend or a family member. Maybe being popular is your god or idol. Or looking perfectly beautiful is what you spend all your time thinking about and trying to make happen. It can really be just about anything at all, and when it becomes an idol in your life—you can tell because nothing else matters except the thing that is getting your whole focus. It can be a good thing (like a family member) or a not-so-good thing (like trying to be perfectly beautiful all the time), but whatever it is, you know it's an idol when God gets shoved out of your life.

I remember a time in my life when I idolized boys and having a boyfriend. I thought about it all the time, and at school, boys were my whole focus. I thought about days as good or bad depending on whether I was able to talk to the boy I liked a

Just think about it. If you understand that what we care about gets our adoration or ongoing attention, see if you can look at your life and figure out if you might be worshipping some things or activities more than you worship God. Now I don't mean that how you spend most of your time is necessarily a signal of what you care about most because the majority of you go to school about seven hours a day, and then you sleep about eight hours a night. No, what I am asking is what takes first place in your heart most

chool. If things were going well with a boy I liked, was happy. If things weren't going well, I was sad. The oys in my life had control over my happiness (though uckily they didn't know it!) because I worshipped hem. And while there is nothing at all wrong with eing attracted to the boys in your life—it's actually quite normal—I was putting far too much focus on hem. They were a good thing in my life that turned nto a bad thing because of idolatry. In this case, boys ook first place, and God tumbled to second or third. Not a good thing.

God doesn't want our whole focus to be on other eople and things. He wants our love and attention.

The Lord God wants first place in our lives, and one of the reasons is because as our Maker he knows what is best for us. He loves us with an everlasting love, and he doesn't like to see us loving things more than we love him because when that happens, our lives turn upside down. We become more and more focused on things other than God, and they end up controlling our lives and breaking our hearts.

So I have a question (if only I could sound like Ryan Seacrest): Do you have what it takes to pray and ask God for help with the problem of idols in your life? Will you allow God to come in and be first place in your life? The truth is, nothing would thrill him more! ✳

JUST BETWEEN US

1. Have you ever really thought about what an idol is and what God says about idolatry? Write out a simple definition of what *idol* means in your own words.

2. Can you look into your own life and locate some possible idols? Write those down next to the definition.

3. How have the idols in your life created problems for you?

4. What steps can you take to keep from worshipping idols in your life?

HOW WELL DO you KNOW YOUR BIBLE FACTS?

by Vicki Courtney

Quiz

Draw a line to match the right person (or people) on the left with the right answer on the right.

Noah

Israelites

Lot's wife

Daniel

Shadrach, Meshach, & Abednego

John the Baptist

12 disciples

Jesus

Jonah

David

Tossed into a lion's den but came out unharmed

Spent some time in the belly of a fish

Wandered for forty years in the wilderness before entering the promised land

Baptized Jesus

A harp-playing, poetry-writing, Goliath-fighting king

Refused to bow down to the king's ninety-foot golden statue and were thrown into a blazing furnace

Never sinned and willingly died on a cross to pay for our sins

Jesus' best friends

Built a giant boat to survive a flood and invited the animals to come aboard

Turned into a pillar of salt

✱ **ANSWERS: Noah:** Built a giant boat to survive a flood and invited the animals to come aboard; **Israelites:** Wandered for forty years in the wilderness before entering the promised land; **Lot's wife:** Turned into a pillar of salt; **Daniel:** Tossed into a lion's den but came out unharmed; **Shadrach, Meshach, and Abednego:** Refused to bow down to the king's ninety-foot golden statue and were thrown into a blazing furnace; **John the Baptist:** Baptized Jesus; **12 disciples:** Jesus' best friends; **Jesus:** Never sinned and willingly died on a cross for our sins; **Jonah:** Spent some time in the belly of a fish; **David:** A harp-playing, poetry-writing, Goliath-fighting king.

god ○ between   135

your instruction manual for living

by Vicki Courtney

Sometimes I hear people joke and say they wish life had come with some sort of instruction manual. Have you ever felt that way? Well, I have good news. It does! God has left us the Bible as our instruction manual. **The Bible contains everything we need to know to make it through life.** Some people will say that it is just a book, that it's nothing special. The Bible is much more than a book. It has the power to change lives.

Listen to what one verse says about the Bible: "All Scripture is inspired by God and is useful to teach us what is true and to make us realize what is wrong in our lives. It straightens us out and teaches us to do what is right. It is God's way of preparing us in every way, fully

> All Scripture is inspired by God. This means that He told the men who wrote the Bible exactly what words to write.

equipped for every good thing God wants us to do (2 Timothy 3:16–17 NLT).

The verse starts by saying that "all Scripture (words in the Bible) is inspired by God." This means that he told the men who wrote the Bible exactly what words to write. Remember that MP3 player? What if it came with

Imagine this. It's your birthday and your family has just gathered in the dining room for a special dinner in your honor. You can barely eat because you're looking at the small pile of presents on the counter, and you are anxious to rip them open. After dinner your mom finally announces it's time for gifts! Excited, you start tearing into them one by one. A new DVD! A new shirt! A new backpack! A new . . . what? What is it? You have just opened a gift that is a total mystery to you. You can tell it plays music—wait, it's an MP3 player! Sweat starts to form on your hands and your heart beats faster. You panic, thinking to yourself, *How will I ever figure this thing out?* Then you see it. There it is lying perfectly flat at the bottom of the box, almost unnoticed. **Behold, the instruction manual.** Immediately, your hands dry up, your heart goes back to normal, and all is right with the world. Now all you have to do is read it!

wo sets of
structions?
What if one
et was written by
kid, and the other
et was written by the
ventor of the MP3 player? Which
ne would you trust? Probably the inventor's instrucon manual, right? The next part of the verse tells us why
od left us the Bible. It teaches us what is true and helps
s know right from wrong. Many of the people who say
he Bible isn't true and inspired by God say that because
hey don't want to admit that some of the things they are
oing are wrong. As Christians, it is very important that
e have some answers as to why we believe the Bible
true and inspired by God. Here are some facts you
eed to know just in case you run across someone
ho thinks the Bible is just a book written by a
unch of men.

ARCHAEOLOGY (ark-ee-all-oh-gee): This big
ord means "the study of really old artifacts." Artifacts
e the things that are left over from cities buried in
he earth from hundreds, even thousands, of years

ago. Have you ever been to a museum and seen dinosaur bones? They are considered artifacts.

For many years artifacts and even cities spoken of in the Bible have been uncovered beneath the earth. For example, a recent study found that the battle of Jericho really happened like it says in the book of Joshua. Remember how Joshua marched around the city seven times and the walls of the city fell in? **Well, archaeologists were digging in that area and found evidence that the walls did tumble down just as the Bible said.** This is just one example. There are more than twenty-five thousand archeological sites (places where things have been found) that have proven things written in the Old Testament (the first part of the Bible).

SCRIPTURE HAS THE SAME MEANING ALL TH[E] TIME: Some people think that because the Bible wa[s] written in a different language and then put into ou[r] language (English), that it may not have the sam[e] meaning today. The Bible was originally written i[n] three languages: Hebrew, Greek, and Aramaic. Ca[n] you understand those languages? No way! Neither ca[n] I! So it makes sense that the Bible has to be put into ou[r] language so we can understand it. The actual meanin[g] of the words in the Bible has not changed; there hav[e] only been small changes in spelling and grammar. Go[d] would want the Bible put into other languages so a[s] many people as possible can understand their instruc[-] tion manual and know how to live their lives.

So there you have it. **You can't ask for a bett[er] or more dependable instruction manual than th[e] Bible.** The only way to know how to live is to rea[d] the manual. Trust me, this is one instruction manu[al] worth reading . . . and rereading and rereading . . . ✳

1. What would you tell a friend who didn't believe in the Bible?

2. How has the Bible helped you to know how to live?

3. If you don't have a Bible, ask your parents or a relative to get you one. When you read it, underline or mark verses that tell you how to live.

Quiz

ARE YOU KIDDING ME?!

by Susie Davis

There are some superstrange stories in the Bible. As a matter of fact, they are so out of this world, upon hearing them you might just say, "Are you kidding me?!" Take the quiz below to see if you know the correct answers to some of the weirder facts in the Bible.

1. The term *read the writing on the wall* comes from:

A) A hand without a body writing on the wall in the Old Testament.

B) The habit of the Israelites to write God's commandments on the walls in their homes.

C) Gang members in the New Testament that were the first to create graffiti.

2. John the Baptist was a prophet who was:

A) Able to talk to animals.

B) Trying to become more popular than Jesus.

C) Killed when a king had his head cut off and placed it on a large party platter.

3. Elijah was a prophet who:

A) Had a beard as long as he was tall.

B) Disappeared into the sky in a chariot and never really died.

C) Breathed fire when he was angry.

4. When Moses brought the Ten Commandments to the Israelites, he:

A) Created a special dance because he was so excited.

B) Dedicated the day and called it Thanksgiving Day.

C) Got so angry that he threw down the tablets, causing God to have to rewrite them.

5. The prophet Balaam had a conversation with talking:

A) Rock

B) Donkey

C) Eagle

6. Moses was known to have:

A) Been buried by God himself.

B) Opened the sky with a lightning rod.

C) Created the first cocoa drink.

ANSWERS:

1. THE CORRECT ANSWER IS A. The phrase "the writing on the wall" comes to us from the book of Daniel when King Belshazzar got freaked out by a hand writing a message on his palace walls. Daniel 5:5–6 says, "At that moment the fingers of a man's hand appeared and began writing on the plaster of the king's palace wall next to the lampstand. As the king watched the hand that was writing, his face turned pale, and his thoughts so terrified him that his hip joints shook and his knees knocked together." Sounds pretty creepy. Read Daniel 5:24–28 for yourself to find out why God wrote the message on the wall.

2. THE CORRECT (ALTHOUGH GRUESOME) ANSWER IS C. Matthew 14:3–12 records: "For Herod had arrested John, chained him, and put him in prison on account of Herodias, his brother Philip's wife, since John had been telling him, 'It's not lawful for you to have her!' Though he wanted to kill him, he feared the crowd, since they regarded him as a prophet. But when Herod's birthday celebration came, Herodias' daughter danced before them and pleased Herod. So he promised with an oath to give her whateve she might ask. And prompted by her mother, she answered, 'Give me John the Baptist's head here on a plat-ter!' Although the king regretted it, he commanded that it be granted because of his oaths and his guests. So he sent orders and had John beheaded in the prison. His head was brought on a platter and given to the girl, who carried it to her mother. Then his disciples came, removed the corpse, buried it, and went and reported to Jesus." Yuck!

3. THE CORRECT ANSWER IS B. Second Kings 2:1 says, "The time had come for the Lord to take Elijah up to heaven in a whirlwind." Then verse 11 says, "As they continued walking and talking, a chariot of fire with horses of fire suddenly appeared and separated the two of them. Then Elijah went up into heaven in the whirlwind." Wonder if that was a holy tornado?

4. THE CORRECT ANSWER IS C. Moses got very angry at the Israelites because of a golden calf they were worshipping, so he destroyed the first copy of the Ten Commandments. Exodus 32:19 says, "As he approached the camp and saw the calf and the dancing, Moses became enraged and threw the tablets out of his hands, smashing them at the base of the mountain." A question for you: How did he make the Israelites pay for their "calf-dancing idolatry"? (Look at Exodus 32:20 for the answer.)

5. THE CORRECT ANSWER IS B. Not only did the donkey talk, but she also saved Balaam's life! God was angry with Balaam because he was making plans outside of God's will. Numbers 22:28–33 records the actual conversation: "Then the Lord opened the donkey's mouth, and she asked Balaam, 'What have I done to you that you have beaten me these three times?' Balaam answered the donkey, 'You made me look like a fool. If I had a sword in my hand, I'd kill you now!' But the donkey said, 'Am I not the donkey you've ridden all your life until today? Have I ever treated you this way before?' 'No,' he replied. Then the Lord opened Balaam's eyes, and he saw the Angel of the Lord standing in the path with a drawn sword in His hand. Balaam knelt and bowed with his face [to the ground]. The Angel of the Lord asked him, 'Why have you beaten your donkey these three times? Look, I came out to oppose you, because what you are doing is evil in My sight. The donkey saw Me and turned away from Me these three times. If she had not turned away from Me, I would have killed you by now and let her live.'" Funny that Balaam never was surprised or frightened by the donkey talking. Bet she was pampered the rest of her sweet little donkey life!

6. THE CORRECT ANSWER IS A. Deuteronomy 34:5–6 says, "So Moses the servant of the Lord died there in the land of Moab, as the Lord had said. He buried him in the valley in the land of Moab facing Beth-peor, and no one to this day knows where his grave is." ✳

Bible ABC's for girls

by Susie Davis

Everyone needs to learn their ABC's. Knowing the alphabet is a must! Here you will find some verses that are important for any girl to know. Read through them and consider making them a part of your everyday thinking by memorizing a few.

A good person produces good words from a good heart and an evil person produces evil words from an evil heart. (Matthew 12:35)

But those who exalt themselves will be humbled, and those who humble themselves will be exalted. (Matthew 23:12)

Come to me, all of you who are weary and carry heavy burdens, and I will give you rest. (Matthew 11:28)

Don't retaliate when people say unkind things about you. Instead, pay them back with a blessing. That is what God wants you to do, and he will bless you. (1 Peter 3:9)

Every word of God proves true. (Proverbs 30:5)

Follow anything that makes you want to do right. (2 Timothy 2:22)

God is not a man that he should lie. He is not a human that he should change his mind. Has he ever spoken and failed to act? Has he ever promised and not carried it through? (Numbers 23:19)

Happy is the person who finds wisdom and gain understanding. For the profit of wisdom is better than silver and her wages are better than gold. Wisdom is more precious than rubies; nothing you desire can compare with her. (Proverbs 3:13–15)

If you believe, you will receive whatever you ask in prayer. (Matthew 21:22)

Just as it is not good to eat too much honey, it is not good for people to think about all the honors they deserve. (Proverbs 25:27)

Keep me from deliberate sins, don't let them control me. (Psalm 19:13)

Lord, you alone are my inheritance, my cup of blessing; you guard all that is mine. (Psalm 16:5)

May he grant you your heart's desire and fulfill all your plans. (Psalm 20:4)

Now I am giving you a new commandment: Love each other. Just as I have loved you, you should love each other. (John 13:34)

O Lord, do not stray away! You are my strength; come quickly to my aid! (Psalm 22:1)

Please, LORD, rescue me! Come quickly, LORD, and help me. (Psalm 40:13)

And without **Q**uestion, the person who has the power to bless is always greater than the person who is blessed. (Hebrews 7:7)

Rather, the Lord's delight is in those who honor him, those who put their hope in his unfailing love. (Psalm 147:11)

Stop your anger! Turn from your rage! Do not envy others—it only leads to harm. (Psalm 37:8)

The one thing I ask of the Lord, the thing I seek most, is to live in the house of the Lord all the days of my life delighting in the Lord's perfections. (Psalm 27:4)

Understanding will keep you safe. Wisdom will save you from evil people, from those whose speech is corrupt. (Proverbs 2:11b–12)

Victory comes from you, O LORD. May your blessings rest on your people. (Psalm 3:8)

We know that those who have become part of God's family do not make a practice of sinning for God's Son holds them securely and the evil one cannot get his hands on them. (1 John 5:18)

e**X**amine yourselves to see if your faith is really genuine. Test yourselves. If you cannot tell that Jesus Christ is among you, it means you have failed the test. (2 Corinthians 13:5)

You care for people and animals alike, O Lord. (Psalm 36:6)

Zeal without knowledge is not good; a person who moves too quickly may go the wrong way. (Proverbs 19:2)

All Bible verses are from the New Living Translation

Quiz

by Susie Davis

POP TEST! WHAT DOES IT TAKE TO BE A CHRISTIAN?

Did you know there is a difference between being a Christian and acting like a Christian? A lot of people can act like Christians, but there's really only one way to be a Christian. What makes someone a Christian? Take this pop quiz and find out!

TRUE OR FALSE . . .

___True   ___False   1. You are a Christian if you go to church.

___True   ___False   2. You are a Christian if you are really nice to other people.

___True   ___False   3. You are a Christian if you pray (even if it is just at mealtimes).

___True	___False	**4. You are a Christian if you obey your parents.**
___True	___False	**5. You are a Christian if you read your Bible.**
___True	___False	**6. You are a Christian if you do good things and are a good person.**
___True	___False	**7. You are a Christian if you confess your sins to God.**
___True	___False	**8. You are a Christian if you memorize Bible verses.**
___True	___False	**9. You are a Christian if your parents are Christians.**
___True	___False	**10. You are a Christian if you believe that Jesus died on the cross for your sins and trust in him to be your Savior.**

ANSWERS: 1–9: FALSE   10: TRUE

If you answered True to any question 1–9, you are not alone. Most people believe that those are the things that make someone a Christian. I know it's hard to understand, but there is a BIG difference between BEING a Christian and ACTING like a Christian. Both are important, but only one is required for you to have eternal life in heaven. Let me explain.

ACTING LIKE A CHRISTIAN

Most of the things listed in questions 1–8 are considered "acting like a Christian." There are a lot of people who act like Christians. Maybe they go to church on Sundays, pray at meals, and even read their Bible every now and then.

However, when you become a Christian, you start to learn more and more about God and the Bible. You begin to realize that the ability to do the things in questions 1–9 comes out of our love for God and our appreciation for his gift of eternal life. In fact, the Bible says that the only reason we have the ability to love other people is because he loved us first! We should act like Christians by living our lives according to what the Bible says.

BEING A CHRISTIAN

When you make the decision to "trust in Jesus," what you are saying is this: "Jesus, I believe that you died on the cross for my sins, and I know that if I believe in you, I can have eternal life in heaven with you. Only you could save me from my sins (be my Savior). I believe there is nothing I can do on my own to earn the right to go to heaven. I want to serve you with my life."

The decision to become a Christian is a choice that only you can make. Your parents can't make it for you. Your pastor/priest can't make it for you. It's up to you. If you would like to become a Christian, be sure to read the next article, "A Hummer of a Deal!" ❋

A HUMMER OF a DEAL

by Vicki Courtney

Can you imagine how excited you would be to find out you won a brand new Hummer? A twenty-five-year-old woman from Los Angeles, California got to experience that excitement—but not for long. The young woman entered a week-long contest sponsored by a local radio station. Listeners were told to add up the number of miles two Hummers traveled around town. The radio would announce where the Hummers were going each day, and people who entered the contest wrote down about how many miles they thought the Hummers traveled from location to location. At the end of the contest, the miles were totaled up and a winner was announced. The young woman arrived at the radio station at 6:00 a.m. to pick up her new Hummer. The day of the giveaway was April 1, 2005. Ring a bell? **You got it—it was nothing more than an April Fools' Day prank.** After arriving at the station and waiting two long hours, a DJ (radio announcer) came out of the station and handed her a radio-controlled toy model of a Hummer. The humiliated young woman is taking the radio station to court and suing them for $60,000 (the cost of a real Hummer) since they tricked her.

Another woman in Kentucky is suing a radio station for a similar joke. The DJ announced that the tenth caller would receive "100 grand." She was the tenth caller, but instead of being awarded $100,000 in cash, she received a 100 Grand brand candy bar. In another April Fools' Day prank, a waitress at a restaurant in Florida won a contest sponsored by the restaurant where the waitresses worked. She and the

> ## iT was noThing MORE Than an APRiL FOOLS' Day PRank!

other waitresses were told that the waitress selling the most beer over a one-month period would receive a Toyota (car). At the end of the month, she was declared the winner, blindfolded, and led out to the parking lot to claim her prize. Unfortunately, when the blindfold was removed, there was no car. In its place was a giant "toy Yoda" Star Wars doll. She sued and won her case. Her lawyer claimed that she won enough money to "pick out whatever type of Toyota she wants."

When you hear about God's offer of forgiveness, you might wonder if it's the real deal or if it's some kind of prank. The truth is that we don't have to earn it, pay for it, or enter a contest to win it. We only have to accept it. Maybe you've heard the saying, "Nothing in life is ever free." Well, **God's gift of forgiveness might be free to us, but it wasn't without cost to God. He sent his one and only Son, Jesus Christ, to die on the cross for our sins.** All those who believe in Jesus Christ and receive God's gift of forgiveness will "win" eternal life (they go to heaven when they die). You might wonder why Jesus had to die. God is perfect and can't be in the presence of anything that is not pure or perfect. When we sin (do things that are wrong), we are not pure, and God cannot be in our presence. But God took care of it when he sent Jesus (someone perfect who had never sinned) to pay the penalty for our sins. He was a pure sacrifice. But here's the cool part: **When you believe in Jesus, he fills your heart. When God looks at you, he doesn't see your sins because Jesus paid the price for them!** They have been forgiven. Now who in the world would refuse an incredible offer like that? Talk about a grand prize—that beats a Hummer any day.

So what about you? Have you claimed your prize of God's forgiveness? That's what it means to be a

TALK ABOUT A GRAND PRIZE! THAT BEATS A HUMMER ANYDAY!

Christian. **Becoming a Christian is the most important decision you will ever make (or not make) in your entire life.** No one can decide for you. You are on your own to decide. If you're not sure if you are a Christian, be sure to read "And the Winner Is . . . You!" You don't want to miss out on this grand prize—it's a real hummer of a deal. ✳

Source:
Foxnews.com Out There; July 16, 2005; www.foxnews.com/story/0,2933,162702,00.html Bummer of a Hummer; LOS ANGELES (AP)

www.snopes.com/business/deals/hummer.asp (Hummer Bummer)

JUST BETWEEN US

1. **Have you claimed your grand prize?**

2. **What is involved in claiming the prize?**

3. **In your opinion, why do you think some people refuse to receive God's offer of forgiveness (the grand prize)?**

4. **When was the last time you told someone about this wonderful prize?**

AND THE WINNER IS... YOU!

by Vicki Courtne[y]

After reading about the grand prize in the article before this one, you might be wondering if you have received God's grand prize of forgiveness. If you are not quite sure if you are a Christian, read what it means to be a Christian below. Remember: this is the most important decision you will ever make in your life. Read very carefully and try to understand what each verse means. Don't worry, we'll take it real slow and go step by step.

WE LEARN ABOUT GOD'S LOVE IN THE BIBLE.

For God so loved the world that he gave hi[s] one and only Son, that whoever believe[s] in him shall not perish but have eternal life —John 3:16 (NIV)

God loves you. He wants to bless your life and mak[e] it happy, full, and complete. He wants to give you a lif[e] that will last forever, even after you die. *Perish* means to di[e] and to be apart from God—forever. God wants you to hav[e] "eternal life" in heaven where you are with him foreve[r]. *If you understand what John 3:16 means, put a check here* —————

WE ARE SINFUL.

For all have sinned; all fall short of God's glori[o]us standard.—Romans 3:23 (NLT)

You may have heard someone say, "I'm only human— nobody's perfect." This Bible verse says the same thing[.] **We are all sinners. No one is perfect. When we sin[,] we do things that are wrong—things that God woul[d] not agree with.** The verse says we fall short of "God[